CARLINES TO
THE COLUMBIA

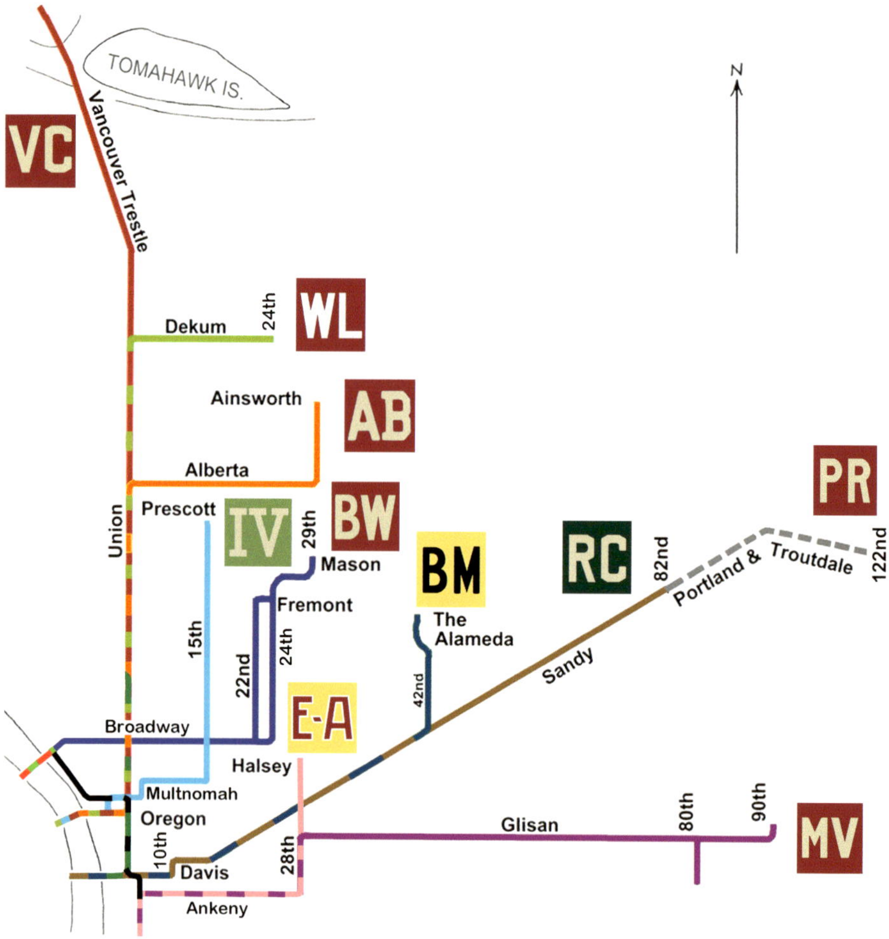
TOMAHAWK IS.
VC
Vancouver Trestle
N
WL
Dekum
24th
AB
Ainsworth
Alberta
Union
Prescott
IV
BW
29th
Mason
Fremont
BM
The Alameda
RC
82nd
PR
Portland & Troutdale
122nd
15th
22nd
24th
42nd
Sandy
Broadway
E-A
Halsey
Multnomah
Oregon
10th
Davis
28th
Ankeny
Glisan
80th
90th
MV

CARLINES TO THE COLUMBIA

THE STREETCARS OF NORTH PORTLAND

RICHARD THOMPSON

AMERICA
THROUGH
TIME

This book is dedicated to streetcar activist
Harry "Larry" Griffith (1914–2004),
who got me started collecting historic streetcar photographs and with whom I served on the Oregon Electric Railway Historical Society board for more than thirty years.

Frontispiece: Twelve streetcar lines served Northeast Portland over the years including (in alphabetical order): Alberta (AB), 1903–1948; Beaumont (BM), 1911–1936; Broadway (BW), 1903–1948; Cloverdale, 1892–1895; East Ankeny (EA), 1892–1913; East 28th (E.28), 1913–1936; Irvington (IV), 1890–1940; Montavilla (MV), 1892–1948; Parkrose (PR), 1911–1928; Rose City (RC), 1907–1936; Vancouver (VC), 1888–1940; Woodlawn (WL), 1900–1937.

Cover image: Alberta car 314 is heading south through the Union Avenue commercial district.

America Through Time®
An imprint of Sutton Publishing Inc.
www.through-time.com

First published 2025

ISBN 978-1-63499-532-0

Typeset in Sabon LT Std
Printed and bound in England

Acknowledgments

I could not have completed my ninth book on the subject of Oregon street and interurban railways without the assistance of fellow local history enthusiasts. In particular, I wish to thank Stephen Kenney Jr., the late Kenn Lantz, Mark Moore, Steve Morgan, Don Nelson, and Wayne Roberts for sharing their knowledge and images.

As with previous volumes, I also want to acknowledge my late friends William K. "Bill" Hayes and G. Charles "Chuck" Bukowsky who were instrumental in turning a simple hobby into a life-changing obsession.

I am also grateful to Steve Morgan and Cameron Booth for proofreading the manuscript. In addition, I am thankful to Cameron for his impressive online database chronicling the history of Portland's streetcar lines, which saved me a lot of period newspaper searching.

Unless otherwise noted, all pictures in this book are from the author's personal collection. Original photographers are cited wherever possible. Further information can be found on the author's website, vintagetrolleys.com.

Contents

Introduction

The area known as Northeast Portland was originally a wilderness of Douglas Fir and Red Cedar trees. It is bounded to the north by land sloping gently down to the Columbia River, and to the east there was once an expanse of meadowland broken by occasional buttes. The west side of Northeast Portland abuts the base of the Portland Peninsula, while E Burnside Street forms the southern border.

For thousands of years, a moderate climate and abundant wildlife made Northeast Portland a comfortable home for indigenous peoples. When the first pioneers arrived, they found the area dotted with Chinookan villages and encampments. There were few Euro-American settlers prior to Congress passing the Donation Land Claim Act in 1850, but the land rush that followed greatly influenced Oregon history. Successive waves of migration brought Irish, Italian, Polish, Russian, Scandinavian, Volga German, and African American residents to this corner of Portland. As the influx continued through the Great Depression and both world wars Northeast Portland gained the most ethnically diverse population in Oregon.

Although the Stark Street Ferry connected Portland to the East Side of the Willamette River in 1855, most early arrivals took up residence on a 2-mile strip of land along the west bank. Significantly, when the Morrison Street Bridge became the first bridge across the river in 1887 it accommodated streetcars as well as pedestrians, horses, and wagons.

Streetcars would play a key role as development spread across the river. Willamette Bridge Railway horsecars began crossing into East Portland and Albina in March 1888 via the Morrison Street Bridge. In November 1889, the first electric streetcars in Oregon began crossing the new Steel Bridge. The Portland & Albina Line trolleys served North Portland, but within months a branch reached Northeast Portland.

Recognition for inaugurating the first mechanically powered streetcar service in Northeast Portland must be awarded to a rival company, however. On July 24, 1888, the Portland & Vancouver Railway Company began laying rails northward through timber and bottomland towards the Columbia River. Lacking bridges, the P&V steam "motor line" would be a portal service linking the ferry terminals for the two cities. Other forms of motive power were also explored. In 1892, the company rejected battery cars in favor of an ill-fated gasoline-electric streetcar that proved unable to pull its own weight. But it did not matter, for within weeks, the bankrupt P&V was taken over by a new company that immediately electrified the system.

As electric streetcars became paramount, tracks headed to the farthest reaches of Northeast Portland. In 1907, Willamette Bridge Railway successor City & Suburban Railway began laying rail alongside an ancient dirt road leading toward the Columbia. Before long, farmland along Sandy Road was being transformed into the largest housing development in Portland. Inside five years, enthusiastic realtors, not content to stop at the city limits, had built a stub line running farther east to the community of Parkrose.

Street railway officials were heavily involved in the housing boom that followed the expanding trolley lines. Among the prominent businessmen promoting real estate development were bridge builders Charles Swigert and Homer Campbell, industrialist Edward Thompson, bankers Frank Dekum and Henry Failing, and entrepreneur William Killingsworth, to name a few. Many of the subdivisions they initiated are still evident today in Alameda Park, Irvington, Piedmont, Rose City Park, Walnut Park, and Woodlawn. Other tracts, with fanciful names like Gleneyrie, Hyde Park, and Merlow have largely faded from memory. Advertisements touting the convenience of a nearby carline promoted housing of all types, from small cottages to English manors.

Streetcar lines did more than spur residential growth, of course. Commercial districts appeared in addition to neighborhoods. During the 1920s, the Hollywood District, named for its historic theater, was Portland's second largest shopping area. Other entertainment and shopping venues reached by local carlines included Irvington and Rose City racetracks, Holladay and Irving parks, Columbia Beach, Jantzen Beach, Lotus Isle, and the commercial districts on Union Avenue (now MLK) and Alberta Street. Numerous schools and churches were also destinations.

At the dawn of the street railway era, Northeast Portland could boast three lines, operated by two competing railway companies. By 1906, when the giant Portland Railway, Light & Power Company merged all railway companies, the number of lines had grown to nine. Four of those remained when the last steel wheel turned in 1948.

Most of the streetcars serving Northeast Portland were housed at the Piedmont Carbarn on N Killingsworth Street, while less modern rolling stock was stored at the old Woodlawn Carbarn on NE Madrona Street. Nearly every type of trolley could be found among their number, including single-truckers, double-truck "Standards," and narrow-gauge interurbans. Many were locally built. Later, multiple-unit, PAYE (pay-as -you-enter), and streamlined cars arrived from national builders. In 1936, trolley buses appeared on the Sandy Boulevard Line.

A dozen carlines can claim to have had terminals here between 1887 and 1948. They connected with nearly every Northeast Portland neighborhood at one time, including Alameda, Beaumont, Concordia, Grant Park, Hollywood, Irvington, King, Rose City Park, Roseway, Sabin, Sullivan's Gulch, Vernon, and Woodlawn. A final chapter celebrates the return of streetcars here, beginning with MAX light rail in 1987. This is the story of those lines.

For additional information, historic car rosters, and line maps, refer to the author's website: vintagetrolleys.com/.

1
Horsecars and Phantom Lines

A problem for modern historians is that Northeast Portland's first streetcar lines were short-lived. Like their brethren in Portland, the first streetcars to operate on the east side of the Willamette River were horse-drawn. They made their appearance in March 1888 one year after the first bridge across the river was opened to the public. The span later known as the Morrison Street Bridge was erected by the Willamette Iron Bridge Company, whose subsidiary railway held the exclusive right to operate streetcars across the new bridge.

Until they merged with Portland in 1891, the east side included the independent towns of East Portland and Albina. It was the goal of the Willamette Bridge Railway Company to build streetcar lines linking all three cities. Accordingly, their first horsecar operation was the Portland & East Portland line.

The Portland & East Portland line was built in stages. In early 1888, rails were laid eastward on "N" Street (now Morrison Street) and then south on 5th Street (now Grand Avenue) to Division Street. Once that had been completed track building commenced northward on Fifth toward Holladay Avenue (now Holladay Street). The collapse of a bridge across Sullivan's Gulch briefly delayed construction, but track laying continued westward on Holladay to N Larrabee Street and the lines were joined in 1889. The extension would later be part of the Holladay Avenue Line.

The first four Willamette Bridge Railway horsecars were single-ended "bobtails" built by the Pullman Company in Illinois. Within weeks, these had been augmented with additional cars, including the largest horsecar in the Northwest, built by the Hammond Company of San Francisco. A major setback occurred on June 30, 1890, when a fire at the stables on "N" and 2nd Streets destroyed the streetcars and killed eighteen horses. Service was restored with horsecars borrowed from the Multnomah Street Railway, but the disaster hastened the abandonment of horse-powered streetcars.

Even after the last Willamette Bridge Railway horsecars had been replaced by trolleys in April 1892, Northeast Portland was not quite finished with horsepower. Two more local horsecar operations were launched, and they operated along different portions of the same street. Their existence, counted in months rather than years, was too brief to leave photographic evidence, so some might call them "phantom" lines.

On July 13, 1892, a new Portland & Vancouver Railway branch opened on what is now NE Killingsworth Street leading from the mainline on Union Avenue (now

MLK) to 25th Street. It began as an extension of the P&V steam motor line; however, a horsecar was substituted when the successor Portland Consolidated Street Railway Company began electrifying the line and converting it to narrow gauge. The horsecar shuttle, named for the Cloverdale neighborhood through which it ran, was replaced by electric streetcars on October 14, 1893. The line had been abandoned by 1895, a victim of Consolidated's bankruptcy.

The last new horsecar line may have also been the shortest lived since there is no further mention of it after it opened. Around 1904, prominent real estate developer William M. Killingsworth is said to have built a short horsecar line as a promotion for his Walnut Park tract. It would have been on his namesake street, running for a few blocks between the NE Union and N Williams Avenue boundaries for his development. For the event, he borrowed horsecar No. 3, which was stored at the Woodlawn Carbarn, and had its dashboards lettered "Killingsworth Ave./Walnut Park." Perhaps he received temporary permission to use tracks then under construction for access to Portland Consolidated Railway's nearby Piedmont Carbarn.

PORTLAND & EAST PORTLAND LINE

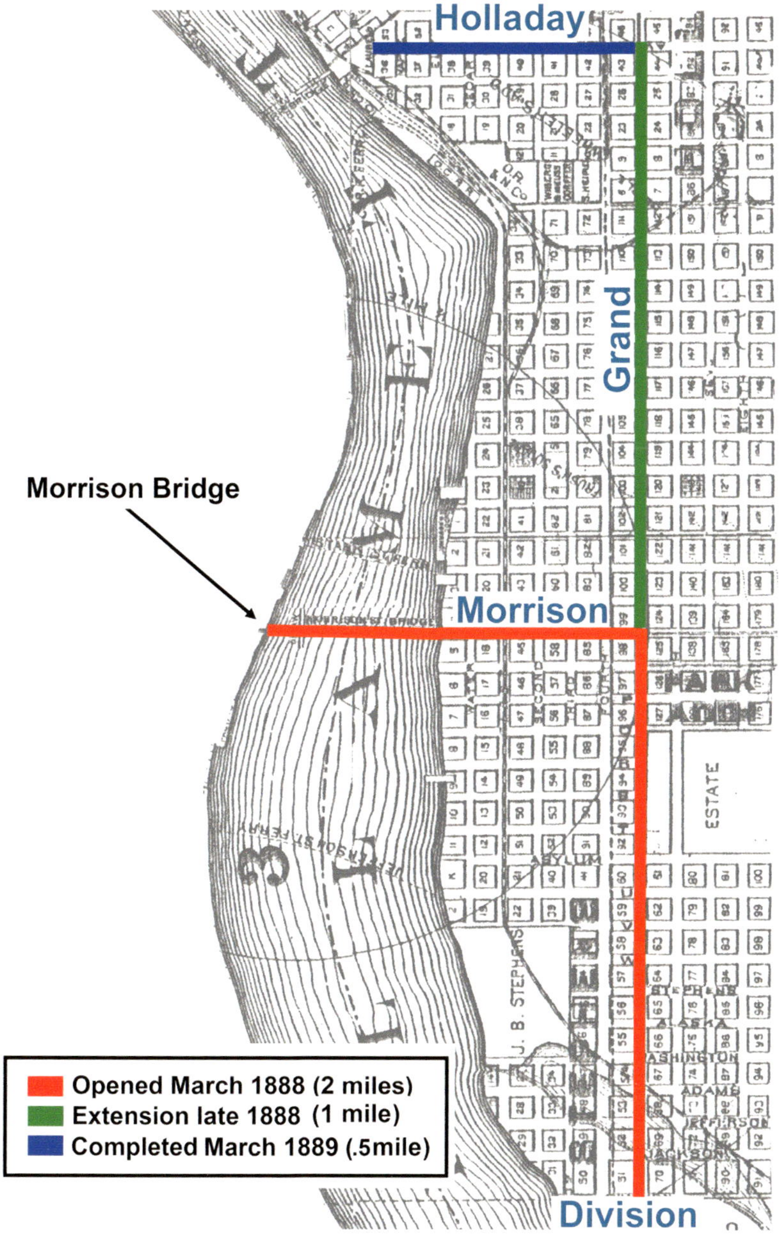

Two Portland & East Portland Line horsecars are meeting at the intersection of Fifth and N Streets (now SE Grand Avenue and Morrison Street) a few months after the Willamette Bridge Railway Company opened the first streetcar line on the east side in March 1888. The initial four cars looked slightly different than the ones seen here because they were single-ended "bob tail" horsecars.

Willamette Bridge Railway horsecars are drawn up in front of the carbarn on N Street (now SE Morrison Street) *c.* 1889. The company wanted to build a steam "motor" line, but the terms of their franchise limited them to becoming the sole horsecar operator on the east side. A disastrous carbarn fire here in June 1890 precipitated conversion to electric streetcar operation.

Although a crude representation, this illustration on the back of a *c.* 1888 Multnomah Street Railway Company 5-cent ticket does show a five-window car with a Bombay roof, the type of vehicle that would have been loaned to the Willamette Bridge Railway Company for use on the Portland & East Portland Line after their fleet of smaller horsecars was destroyed in the June 1890 carbarn fire. (*Courtesy Don Nelson*)

Multnomah Street Railway No. 1 is seen in front of the carbarn on 13th (now SW 16th Avenue) and Washington Streets in November 1882. Unlike earlier horsecars, Multnomah's were large, double-ended cars, some of which were built locally. This was the type of vehicle loaned to the Willamette Bridge Railway Company after their East Portland carbarn burned in 1890. (*Courtesy Mark Moore*)

One of the three Columbia Land & Improvement Company horsecars is seen in what appears to be a *c.* 1889 builder's photograph from Pullman's Palace Car Company in Illinois. Columbia Land & Improvement operated horsecar lines in Vancouver, Washington, from the Columbia River ferry landing to Vancouver Heights and the Vancouver barracks. The horsecars were replaced in late 1892 when successor Portland Consolidated Street Railway electrified the Vancouver operation.

After trolleys replaced the horsecars in Vancouver during the summer of 1892, they were used as trailers behind the electric cars until new owner Portland Consolidated Street Railway Company shipped them back across the Columbia River, where they likely saw temporary use on the Cloverdale line that ran along NE Killingsworth Street from Fourth (now MLK) to 23rd Streets. Afterward, the cars deteriorated during years of storage at the old Woodlawn carbarn, and later the Piedmont Carbarn.

HORSECAR STUB LINES

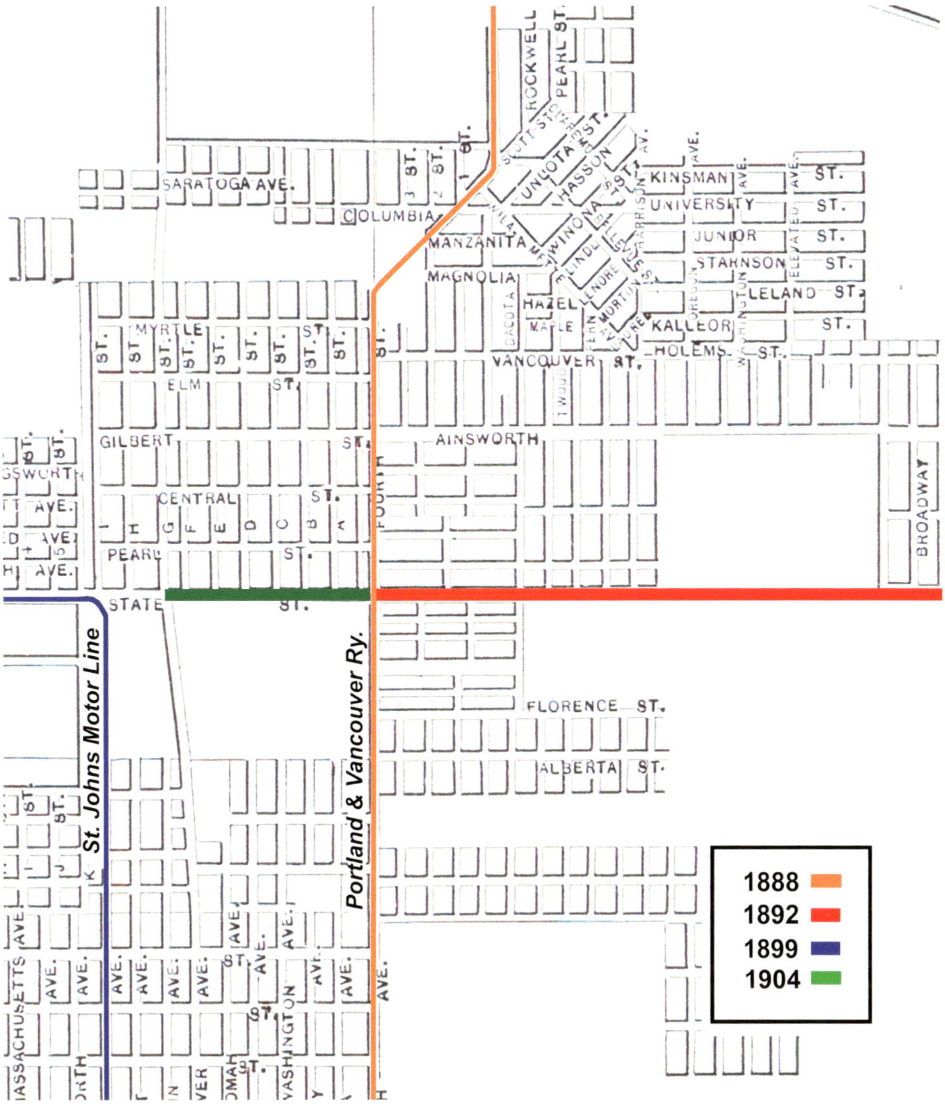

Little is known about Portland's last new horsecar lines except that they were short-lived stub lines. The terminals for both the Cloverdale and Walnut Park lines were located on 4th Street (later Union Avenue and now MLK). Their routes, highlighted in red and green, have been added to this detail from Habersham, Nieberding & Tarbet's 1891 City of Portland Map. Note: By the time the horsecar lines opened "State Street" had become Killingsworth Street, and the short Killingsworth Street located four blocks to the north became Holman Street.

Columbia Land & Improvement horsecar No. 3 was brought out of retirement in 1904 when businessman William M. Killingsworth borrowed it to promote his Walnut Park development. It travelled along his eponymous street with dashboards reading "Killingsworth Avenue" and "Walnut Park." For a time afterwards, No. 3 may have become a summerhouse next to the Killingsworth home seen here on N Alberta Avenue.

Driver Richard G. Sloan posed with horsecar No. 3 for this January 18, 1934, photo at the Portland Travel and Transportation Exposition. Sloan, who was working as a motorman on the Vancouver Line at the time, was chosen for this assignment because he drove horsecars on the Metropolitan Railway Company's 2nd Street Line when he began working in 1894. (*Morning Oregonian photograph*)

In this publicity photo taken at the Center Street Shops, Attorney Joseph K. Carson and three unidentified officials are posing aboard a very tired-looking No. 3 (the number is barely visible on the dash). They are celebrating the arrival of the new Mack buses in the background whose purchase was made possible by the twenty-year franchise granted to Portland Traction Company in 1936. (*Courtesy Oregon Historical Society*)

The horses refused to drink from the historic Skidmore Fountain on SW 1st Avenue and Ankeny Street as No. 3 made ready to lead the parade celebrating completion of the Front Avenue Project on November 21, 1942. At the helm is Alexander "Alex" Aitken and holding the horses is Paul "Gus" Buchholz. Both men started working on City & Suburban Railway horsecars in 1891 at the age of fourteen. (*Oregonian photograph*)

Around 1940 the letters "P.E.P.CO" were added to the sides of No. 3, as can be seen in this parade at the corner of SE Hawthorne Boulevard and 50th Avenue. Portland Traction Company continued operations but both city and interurban lines were now part of the Portland Electric Power holding company. No. 3 had become a slave to public relations, appearing in celebrations throughout town. (*Courtesy Don Nelson*)

In 1948, Portland Traction Company Superintendent of Equipment Earl B. Richardson purchased horsecar No. 3 and placed it in his backyard. A year later, he donated it to the Milwaukie Historical Society, who displayed it in a park on McLoughlin Boulevard and Jefferson Street in Milwaukie for five years. The "P.E.P.CO." letters were now covered by a fresh coat of paint. (*Courtesy Mark Moore*)

In 1953, the Milwaukie Historical Society loaned Oregon's oldest streetcar to a policemen's fraternal organization called the Portland Footprinters. Footprinter Damon J. Trout then had it "restored" as Portland Street Railway No. 3 for operation on his WOD & DJT Railroad (named after Trout and his friend U.S. Chief Justice William O. Douglas) in North Plains. He is seen here in a Milwaukie parade on July 24, 1954, prior to No. 3 being moved to Trout's Rancho Marelco estate.

Information on the reverse of this postcard showing No. 3 in front of the Milwaukie Historical Society describes it as a Portland Street Railway horsecar dating from 1872. However, in 1958, historian David L. Stearns lamented, "that is entirely erroneous" since it was a Pullman product and that company's first streetcars were manufactured in 1889. He explained that, in spite of the fine rebuilding by Damon Trout, the historic car was of a completely different type than that used on the Portland Street Railway.

2
The Vancouver Line

During the spring of 1888, as work was nearing completion on the second span to cross the Willamette River, two competing companies raced to build street railway systems to the east side, one of which would be mechanized. First place went to the Willamette Bridge Railway, whose horsecars were soon operating across the Morrison Street Bridge and the new Steel Bridge. However, by July 1888, the Willamette Bridge Railway's Mount Tabor Steam "Motor" Line was meeting the horse-drawn streetcars at what is now SE 5th and Morrison Streets.

But the Willamette Bridge Railway would not gain all the accolades. That same July, the Portland & Vancouver Railway Company began laying rails northward through timberland toward the Columbia River. A group of Portland businessmen headed by Frank Dekum incorporated the P&V on April 27, 1888, to build a railway linking the Stark Street and Vancouver ferry terminals. Along the way it would cross through Woodlawn, an area being developed by the Oregon Land & Investment Company, which owned the railway.

The Portland & Vancouver Railway began as a 3-foot gauge steam railway. A typical train consisted of two passenger coaches pulled by a small locomotive known as a "dummy" because the engine was hidden inside a car body resembling a streetcar. The little engines circumvented an East Portland ordinance prohibiting steam locomotives on city streets. Even so, the inaugural trip on September 16, 1888, had to be made aboard two flatcars hauled by a construction locomotive. The first locomotive and passenger car, products of San Francisco's Phoenix Iron Works and John Hammond & Company, had proved incompatible with the railway's tight curves and trestlework. In early 1889, they were augmented with two Baldwin steam motors and matching Pullman Palace Car Company coaches. Additional rolling stock included the former Oregonian Railway parlor car "Lady Maude" and a boxcar nicknamed the "beer car" since it was often used to haul product from Henry Weinhard's Vancouver Brewery.

Steam motors proved a temporary expedient for the Portland & Vancouver Railway. On April 23, 1892, three weeks after a fatal steam motor accident, new owner Portland Consolidated Street Railway Company began to convert the Vancouver Line to electric operation and regauge it to 42 inches. In 1906, it became part of the Portland Railway, Light & Power Company, who commenced operating over 3 miles of new trestlework and private right-of-way to Hayden Island.

The Vancouver Line was very successful over the years, particularly after the Interstate Bridge replaced the Vancouver Ferry in 1917. A variety of equipment, from the locally built narrow-gauge combination cars nicknamed "Vancouvers," to the first large-vestibuled "pay-as-you-enter" (PAYE) streetcars, were assigned to the route. Along the way, many passengers would get off at Columbia Beach during the 1910s, and at the Lotus Island or Jantzen Beach amusement parks during the 1930s. In spite of these popular entertainment venues, Portland Traction Company discontinued the Vancouver Line on September 8, 1940.

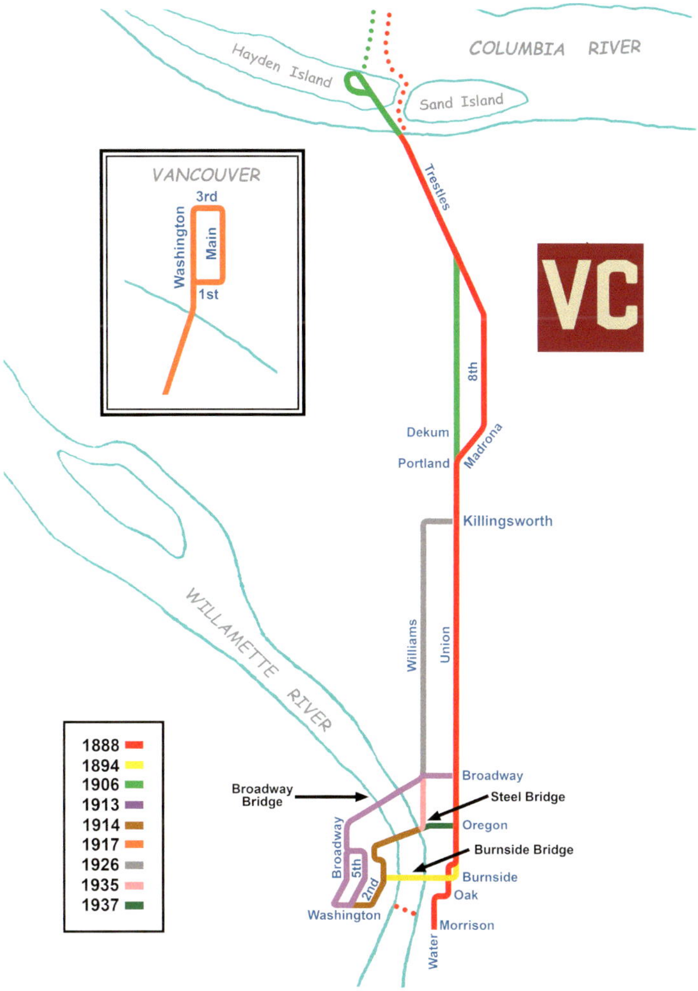

The Portland terminus for the Vancouver Line changed several times over the years. The steam motor met the Stark Street Ferry. As new bridges were built across the Willamette River, trolleys would utilize three different spans. At the other end of the line, two ferry landings were used prior to completion of the Interstate Bridge in 1917. There was a track loop at Hayden Island Station. Line length to Hayden Island was approximately 8 miles. To Vancouver, 12.

Portland & Vancouver Railway steam motor No. 2 and two Pullman coaches are at the southern end of the line on SE Water Street next to the Stark Street Ferry landing in 1892. The festive occasion is unknown, but it may have been the merger with the Portland Consolidated Street Railway on May 26.

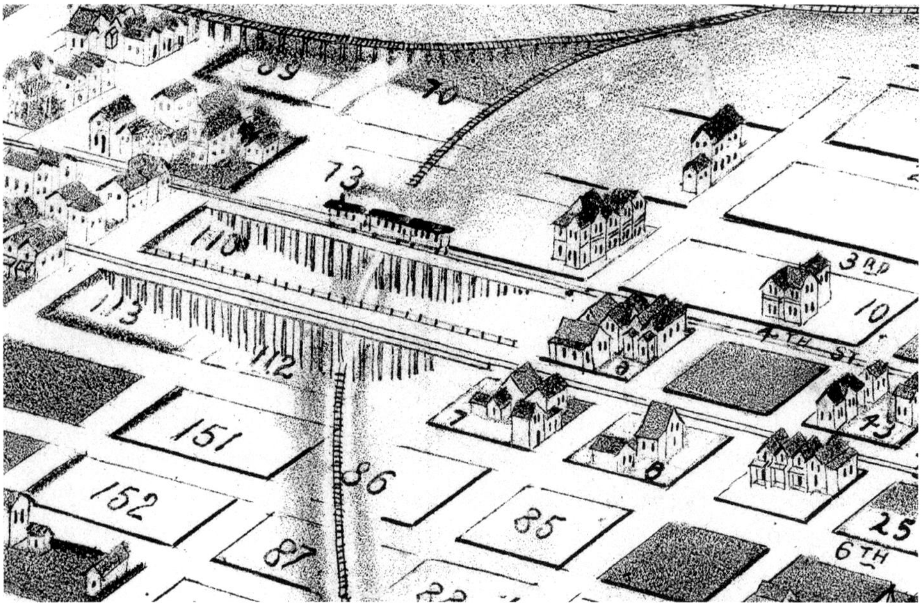

This detail from the Oregon Real Estate Company's charming hand-drawn 1891 map of Holladay's Addition depicts a typical Portland & Vancouver Railway steam motor train crossing the Fourth Street (soon renamed Union Avenue) trestle over Sullivan's Gulch. The southbound train is one mile from its terminus on SE Water Street.

Excessive speed caused by a broken throttle resulted in this derailment on the curve at Union Avenue (now MLK Boulevard) and NE Couch Street. Escaping steam scalded engineer John Hans, who died two days later. The wreck occurred on April 4, 1893, three weeks before the Vancouver Line was electrified.

This photograph was taken on June 24, 1893, the last day for steam motor operation on the Portland & Vancouver Railway. The location was Highland Station, which was located near what is now NE MLK Boulevard and Going Street. Dummy engine No. 2 is pulling a passenger coach and a combination passenger and freight car.

In January 1892, the Multnomah Street Railway Company ordered six double-truck streetcars from the J. G. Brill Company for its Washington Street line. After acquiring the Portland & Vancouver Railway Company, these cars were reassigned, becoming the "Vancouver Forties," the first trolleys on the newly electrified Vancouver Line.

Opposite page: The "Vancouver Forties" were considered large cars at the time since they could accommodate thirty-two passengers. Note the gothic windows, fabric-covered wooden bench seats, and advertisement cards for products such as Old Forester Whisky, Olympic Flour, Grape-Nuts cereal, and Knabe pianos. Spliced horsecar No. 155 can be seen inside the Woodlawn Carbarn in the center background.

OLD FORESTER

A lone carman looks toward the camera as snowplow-equipped motorized flatcar No. 908 makes ready to clear the tracks for Vancouver Line car 192. In 1906, Portland Railway Company built narrow-gauge interurbans 600–603 as combines with rear freight compartments. By 1912, renumbered in the 191 class, they were regularly assigned to the Vancouver run, which gained them the moniker "Vancouvers."

The "Vancouvers" usually operated in tandem with 350-class Fuller trailers. Both car types were locally built around 1905 at the Washington Street Carbarn. Cars 191 and 351 are seen here at a trestle approach on the Vancouver Line with motorman Edward Hooks and conductors Jacob Peters and Ray Goodwin. The Nelson Safety Fender means this picture was taken after 1913.

Motorman Ralph Ryan and conductor Carl Behm are posing with cars 192 and 351 on the loop track at Hayden Island Station, which included the lunchroom seen in the background. This was the northern terminus of the Vancouver Line. The Vancouver Ferry landing was located down the hill to the left of the station. (*Courtesy Mark Moore*)

Since 1891, the railway company had operated the ferry to Vancouver, but the days were numbered for the PRL&P ferry "City of Vancouver" when this photograph was taken in 1917. The postcard caption reads, "Pacific Highway Interstate Bridge length including approaches 4 miles, making it one of the longest steel bridges in the world." The bridge toll for automobiles was 5 cents. (*Courtesy Mark Moore*)

Crowded Fuller trailer No. 354 is on the tail end of a Vancouver Line train as it heads back across the Columbia River over the new Interstate Bridge in this vintage postcard scene. In 1958, a nearly identical vertical lift span bridge was added alongside the first bridge. The "Limited" dash sign means this is an express making fewer stops. (*Courtesy Mark Moore*)

The motorman and conductors required for a two-car train are proudly posing with motor 194 and trailer 354 at Third and Main Streets in downtown Vancouver not long after the Interstate Bridge opened. Interestingly, a 241-class Fuller open car is close behind, but it is not part of the same train. Three-car trains were rarely seen on the Vancouver Line. (*Courtesy Mark Moore*)

By the 1930s, two-car trains had disappeared from the Vancouver Line. Now the "Vancouvers" were operating singly, supplemented by traditional city trolleys like No. 273, seen here on the Interstate Bridge. Car 273 began life as a "Council Crest Open" but was enclosed in 1918. The 260–273 series were seldom seen in Northeast Portland until after the Savier Carbarn in Northwest Portland was closed in 1936.

No. 193, seen on a bright 1930s day at Third and Main Streets in Vancouver, was once a combine, but early on the freight compartment was converted for use as a smoker. Although the 191–194 series had controls at both ends, they always ran as single-enders with the former freight compartment at the rear. The dash advertising sign is for G. G. Gerber Auto Repairs and Rebuilding on NW Glisan Street in Portland.

A two-car Vancouver Line train made up of combine 191 and Fuller trailer 351 races across the Columbia Slough bridge in 1909. Three years previously Portland Railway, Light & Power Company had rebuilt trestles in order to extend the tracks to utilize the ferry terminal on Hayden Island instead of Switzler's Landing. Note the boat rental business below the bridge. (Note: colorization by the author.)

Vancouver Line trolleys traversed more than 2,500 feet of trestles and private right-of-way across Columbia River bottomland. Here, No. 273 is seen passing Vancouver-bound car 192 on the trestle near Faloma Station. Faloma is an acronym derived from the first two letters of the last names of three riverboat officers who owned land in this area: Captain Farnsworth, Captain Love, and Engineer Maier.

Passengers peer from the open windows as northbound Vancouver Line car 193 scurries across a trestle on a warm day in 1936. Notice that the Nelson Safety Fenders are gone, having been replaced by experimental Portland Railway fenders in 1927. Another modification to these former combines came in 1933 when train doors were cut into the freight ends of each car. (*Charles Hayden photograph*)

Vancouver Line car 402 is northbound at the passing track above N Columbia Boulevard during the late 1930s. The "Front Entrance" designation on the VC dash sign is evidence of Portland Traction Company having converted to one-man operation. The Vancouver Line was almost entirely single-track north of Union Avenue, but there were four passing tracks. (Note: colorization by the author.)

Car 403 is travelling over private right-of-way near the Columbia River on a July evening in 1939. The 400–439 series were the only narrow-gauge streetcars equipped with multiple-unit control. As such, they were semi-permanently coupled in two-car trains during the early years and assigned to replace the larger interurban-style cars on the St. Johns and Vancouver lines. Why is the motorman holding a bucket?

All the windows are open as No. 403 rolls down Union Avenue in the late 1930s. Note the designation for "Jantzen Beach" above the VC dash sign. In 1929, the station stop for "Hayden Island" was discontinued. The station would now be designated "Jantzen Beach," in recognition of the popular amusement park that opened on Hayden Island on May 26, 1928.

No. 482's apple green and cream livery glows in the sun as it rests at Faloma Station. The 466–485 series trolleys were the first to have large PAYE (pay-as-you-enter) vestibules. The community of Faloma was settled in 1907 when a one-room schoolhouse was built. Faloma Station was also called Lotus Isle Station from 1930 to 1932, the years in which the amusement park operated.

Vancouver Line streetcars carried passengers to several recreation and entertainment venues. The first of these was Columbia Beach, which was developed as a camping and picnic spot by Portland Railway, Light & Power Company. It was located on Sand Island (renamed Tomahawk Island in 1927). The photograph above was taken in 1918. (*Courtesy Mark Moore*)

A popular family destination was Jantzen Beach, which opened in 1928. The Venetian Canal Ride was added in 1931. Other attractions included the dance pavilion in the background, as well as swimming pools, a fun house, the Big Dipper roller coaster, and C. W. Parker Carousel. The park closed in 1970 after years of decline and the buildings were razed to build a shopping center. (*Courtesy Stephen Kenney Jr.*)

On June 28, 1930, the former site of Columbia Beach was transformed into a "Million-Dollar Pleasure Paradise" named Lotus Isle. Portland's largest, and some say creepiest, amusement park encompassed 128 acres on Tomahawk (formerly Sand) Island east of Jantzen Beach. The most macabre looking of the park's forty attractions must have been "The Bulldog," which housed the bumper cars. (*Courtesy Mark Moore*)

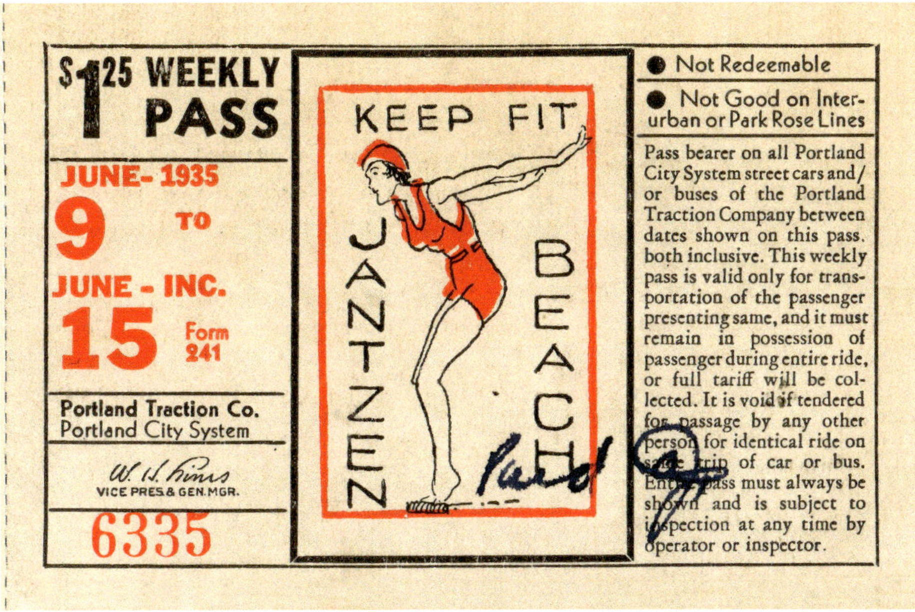

Jantzen Beach Amusement Park is featured on this June 1935 Portland Traction Company weekly pass. Commuters could save money by buying a monthly pass for $1.25 instead of paying each time they rode. Riders on the Vancouver Line would have paid the regular city zone fare of 6 cents up to the city limits, and then another 5 cents if riding on to Jantzen Beach, or an additional 9 cents if going to Vancouver.

A single passenger waits as Vancouver car 482 makes ready to depart Jantzen Beach Station. During the Great Depression, fewer people could afford to visit amusement parks. The dash advertisement is for Wolfard Ford & Mercury Service, which was located on Grand Avenue in Portland. (*Courtesy Mark Moore*)

No. 483 lays over on 3rd and Washington in Vancouver in 1939, a little over one year from the end of service. On this hot July 9th, the motorman has opened nearly every window in the car to cool it down before departure. The McCoy Auto Garage building is in front of the streetcar.

Car 484 is rumbling northbound past Pioneer Automotive on Washington Street in Vancouver. The lone Interstate Bridge can be seen in the background. There were only a few more days of service for the Vancouver Line, but not for the car. After the VC line closed on September 3, 1940, trolley 484 was transferred to the Ankeny Division in Southeast Portland, where it continued working for eight more years.

3
The Irvington Line

While street railway tracks spread north to the Columbia River, and eastward beyond city limits, three lines were being built into the heart of Northeast Portland. In some places, trolleys on these inner Northeast routes passed within blocks of each other. Whereas in other parts of town industry grew alongside streetcar lines this was seldom the case here. The primary commercial activity along carlines in Northeast Portland was the grading of hillsides and filling in of gullies for the development of new residential tracts.

Work on the state's first electric streetcar operation began even before completion of the horsecar line on 5th Street (Grand Avenue) in East Portland. In late 1888, the Willamette Bridge Railway was granted an exclusive franchise across the new Steel Bridge and horsecars began accessing that second span across the Willamette River as soon as rails were laid on Holladay Avenue. By July 1889, as electrification extended northward into Albina from the bridge approach, a branch line into the Irvington tract was also planned.

The Portland & Albina Line to North Portland garnered all the attention when it opened on November 4, 1889, but it would soon gain a sibling in Northeast Portland. Trolley service out Holladay and Multnomah streets to what is now NE 15th Avenue and Hancock Street opened in the autumn of 1890. Successor company City & Suburban Railway added an extension to the line on NE Tillamook Street to 19th that was later dropped in favor of continuing northward on 15th. The route was briefly called the Holladay Line in reference to Holladay's Addition, through which it passed. However, by 1902 it had been designated the Irvington Line.

In 1914, Portland Railway, Light & Power combined the Irvington Line with Southwest Portland's Depot & Jefferson Line, creating a new downtown terminus for the Irvington cars. Irvington-Jefferson streetcars ran along the SW 5th Street route that had once been the domain of cable cars, providing riders with access to shopping while also linking them with the Goose Hollow neighborhood. I-J trolleys alternated between a southern terminus on SW Jefferson and Stout streets (20th Avenue) and one on Chapman Street (18th Avenue) and Mill Street at the foot of the old cable incline. A final change came in 1933, when the branch to SW Jefferson and 20th Avenue was discontinued and the line name became just Irvington again.

The original equipment assigned to the Irvington Line consisted of smaller 100-series streetcars. After the turn of the twentieth century, Irvington passengers were riding on longer trolleys like those in the 400-class. The most modern rolling stock to appear on the Irvington run were the 521-class PAYE cars that arrived during the 1910s. All operated out of the Piedmont Carbarn in North Portland.

Until 1908, a maximum of three streetcars were required to maintain schedules on the Irvington Line. After 1911, this had increased to five. The Irvington Line was converted to bus operation on August 17, 1940.

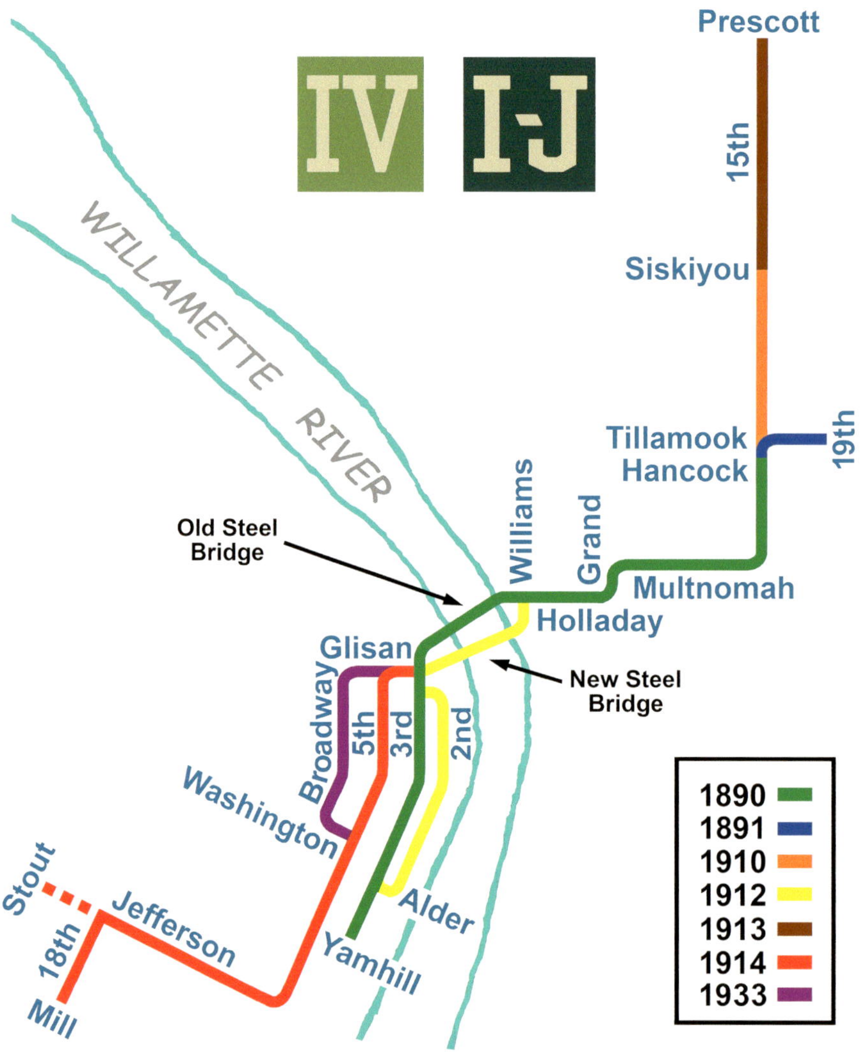

The Irvington Line dates from 1890, when the Willamette Bridge Railway Company established the second electric streetcar line to serve Northeast Portland. As can be seen on this map both east and west terminals changed several times during the line's fifty years of existence. The only thing that remained constant was that the Steel Bridge (old and new) was used to cross the Willamette River except during periods of construction. The line length was approximately 4 miles.

The crew of City & Suburban Railway car 28 are watching the camera during an 1890s layover at the early terminus of the Irvington Line on what would now be NE Tillamook Street at 19th Avenue. A bay-windowed "portable vestibule" has been attached to No. 28, which was one of three cars ordered from the Northern Car Company in Minneapolis to open service on the line. It was scrapped in 1911.

Several interesting details can be seen in this view of City & Suburban Railway No. 48 at the Irvington Line terminus on NE Tillamook Street. Instead of a uniform hat the conductor is wearing a straw boater, and a small fare register is slung over his shoulder. Note the window shutters and the unabbreviated dash sign. Spliced horsecar 48, renumbered 164, burned in a 1910 fire at the Piedmont Carbarn.

City & Suburban Railway No. 63 was one of the former white and gold-painted trolleys built by the Pullman Company in 1891. It is seen here at the NE Tillamook and 19th Street Irvington Line terminal in the early 1900s. Although stripped of motors in 1917, car 63, renumbered 179 by Portland Railway, Light & Power Company, was not officially retired until 1923.

Car 120 was built in the City & Suburban Railway's Savier Street shops around 1894. Later known as the "C & S Standards," the forty-seven cars in the 100–146 series comprised the largest car type operated by the C&S. The "Standards" followed the company's successful rebuilding of spliced horsecars. No. 120 is seen at the Irvington terminal prior to 1910 during the PRL&P years. (*Courtesy Steven Kenney Jr.*)

Irvington Addition was platted in 1887, but development did not get underway until the 1890s following the arrival of the streetcar. As can be seen in this contemporary postcard Irvington became a desirable neighborhood with many stately homes built on large lots. Building of middle- to upper-class homes began to slow down during the 1910s due to competition from developments in Rose City Park and Laurelhurst.

In 1887, the Portland Driving Park Association opened Irvington Racetrack on land now occupied by Irving Park. The Irvington streetcar passed within a couple of blocks of the track, providing convenient access. Today this is one of two Northeast Portland parks that once contained racetracks. This Oregonian photograph was taken on July 5, 1907, the last year of operation for the track.

Although cropped, this picture is interesting because it shows the operation of a former Portland Railway Company Fuller car on the Irvington Line. Records indicate this type of car was not assigned to the Irvington run until 1911, which means the photo can be dated as having been taken between then and 1913 when the last of 1,200 Nelson Safety Fenders had been installed. (*Photo courtesy Mark Moore*)

In February 1914, the Portland Railway, Light & Power Company combined the Irvington and Jefferson streetcar lines. Cars now alternated between SW Stout and Mill Streets in Portland, while the other end of the line had been extended to NE 15th and Prescott the previous August. I-J PAYE car 566 was built in 1909 by the American Car Company.

Right: Irvington car 644 appears to be snowbound during the Big Snow of 1916, which paralyzed Portland transportation. The picture is not a great one, but it does give some indication of conditions in which carmen were expected to stay with their trolley until the weather improved. No. 664 was one of the 144 PAYE cars built by the American Car Company between 1909 and 1911 in St. Louis.

Below: No. 251 was one of the series riders nicknamed "pneumonia cars" because around 1906 these former open cars were hastily enclosed without bulkheads or heaters. Irvington-Jefferson trolley 251 is outbound at N Williams Avenue and Oregon Street in 1925 with the Steel Bridge approach in the background. The dash advertisement promotes the Gilda Gray movie *She'll Shake the Town* at the Columbia Theater.

Inbound car 425 rolls slowly past the Pioneer Post Office and Meier & Frank department store on SW 5th and Morrison Street as it heads for the western I-J line terminus on SW Jefferson Street. The year is 1927 and the city appears to be getting ready for the Rose Festival. Because of a supposedly rough ride, 400 series cars were not popular with some passengers.

Eastbound car 424 is on NE Multnomah Street approaching 15th Avenue after the I-J line name had reverted to Irvington in 1933. Today the Lloyd Center Mall is located behind the trolley. Although Ralph Lloyd acquired most of Holladay's Addition between 1923 and 1933 for a proposed east side civic center, the area would remain vacant until the shopping mall was built in 1960.

Passengers are dressed in their "go to town" attire as Irvington car 425 approaches the intersection of NW 15th Avenue and Broadway. Perhaps it is Sunday, or riders may be headed for the nearby shopping district typified by the single-level market in the background. Note that seating on these attractive 1907 vintage trolleys was on longitudinal bench seats.

This shot of No. 433 was taken at exactly the same spot as sister 425 in the previous picture, perhaps at the same time. The weather remains nice, and the car is crowded with commuters and shoppers. The two pictures are similar except for the paint colors. Car 425 wears the apple green and cream livery introduced in the 1930s, whereas No. 433 sports the traditional dark red and cream paint scheme.

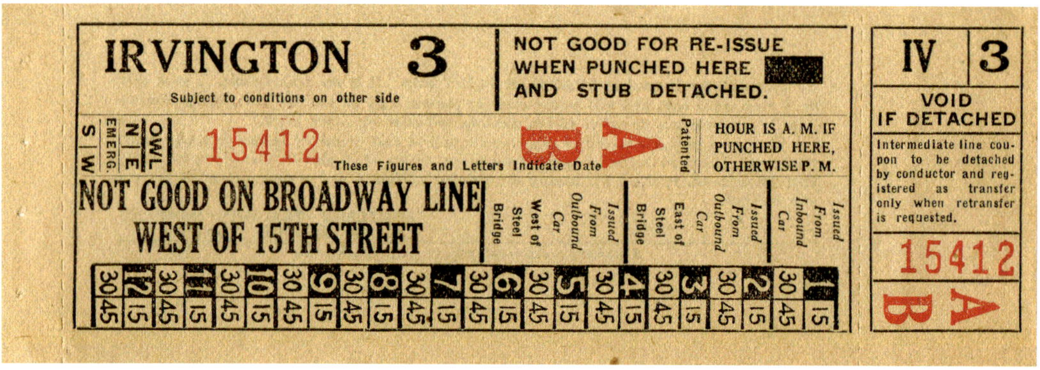

This unused Irvington Line transfer is from the 1930s. Among the clutter of details are spaces for inbound and outbound streetcars crossing the Steel Bridge as well as the warning that it was, "not good on Broadway line west of 15th street." The back side bears the name of W. H. Lines, who became Portland Traction Company's vice president in 1933.

This latter-day picture of Irvington streetcar 419 was taken at the outer end of the line, which was then NE 15th Avenue and Prescott Street. The operator has changed ends and is enjoying a moment's relaxation before departure. Car 419 remained in use long after discontinuation of Irvington service, but the dented dash suggests deferred maintenance. Note the modern "bus driver" style cap.

4

The East Ankeny and Montavilla Lines

The East Ankeny Line cannot be categorized by a single geographical district because it served two. Like the majority of the city's streetcar lines it followed a radial pattern, extending from the city center like the spokes of a wheel. However, while most of its route ran through Northeast Portland, East Ankeny and its successor also had terminals in Southeast Portland.

The Portland & Fairview Railway Company was incorporated on September 19, 1890, to build a steam motor line from the end of the City & Suburban Railway's Mount Tabor Line at what is now SE 54th Avenue and Belmont Street to NE 95th Avenue and Glisan Street in what was then considered part of the community of Fairview. The company awarded the C&S a subsidy to build and operate the "Fairview Road," but when construction commenced, officials had been persuaded to build their railway from a different terminal. It would now run from NE Glisan Street to 82nd Avenue. More importantly, when the East Glisan Line opened in 1892 it would be an electric stub line rather than a steam railway. By the time C&S purchased the operation in 1899, it had become part of the East Ankeny Line.

The City & Suburban Railway Company started construction of the East Ankeny Line in 1892. This slightly later start allowed it to use electric streetcars, which gave the line an advantage over the steam "motors" chugging over the Mt. Tabor Line six blocks to the south. On July 26, 1892, the C&S inaugurated East Ankeny Line service to NE 28th and Couch Streets. At that time, the company was also in the process of building the line on NE Glisan Street.

In 1900, the East Glisan terminus was relocated from an empty field at NE 82nd and Glisan to what is now SE 80th Avenue and Stark Streets. Since the new alignment went to the Mount Tabor Villa development, the line was renamed. Too lengthy for trolley signs, it was abbreviated "Mt. Ta. Villa," then "Monta.Villa," and finally "Montavilla." The community's name, inherited from a trolley sign, remains in use today.

Things become a bit murky for the modern historian around 1903, when the East Ankeny Line was extended from the carbarn at E 28th and Couch Street to what is now NE 28th Avenue and Halsey Street. It was known as the East 28th Street Line. However, the original "EA" line was still listed in streetcar directories and four years later it began sharing a new extension on Sandy Road from NE 28th to 67th Street with the new Rose City Park Line.

In 1911, cutbacks hastened the demise of the two East Ankeny Line branches. The northern branch now terminated at NE 28th and Sandy Road, while the southern route ran over a portion of the Montavilla Line to NE 39th and Glisan Street in Laurelhurst.

The year 1911 also brought change to the Montavilla Line. A branch was built from what is now NE 80th Avenue and Glisan Street to NE 90th Avenue and Irving Street, where passengers could transfer to the Mt. Hood Railway. MV cars now had two east side terminals, SE 80th and Stark in Montavilla, and NE 90th and Irving.

In May 1913, both East Ankeny Line services were discontinued and the East 28th Street Line became a stub line operating on 28th Street between NE Glisan and Halsey streets, where most of its riders were employees of the Doernbecher Furniture plant, which was described at the time as "The biggest furniture factory under one roof in the world."

During the first years of operation, equipment assigned to the East Ankeny and Montavilla lines consisted mainly of C&S 100-class "Standards," and Portland Railway 450 series "Torontos." In 1910, large PAYE 500s appeared. Eleven cars were required to maintain service in 1907, which increased to twenty-five cars by 1913. In 1936, the East 28th Street stub line was discontinued. The Montavilla Line continued until gasoline buses replaced streetcars on August 1, 1948.

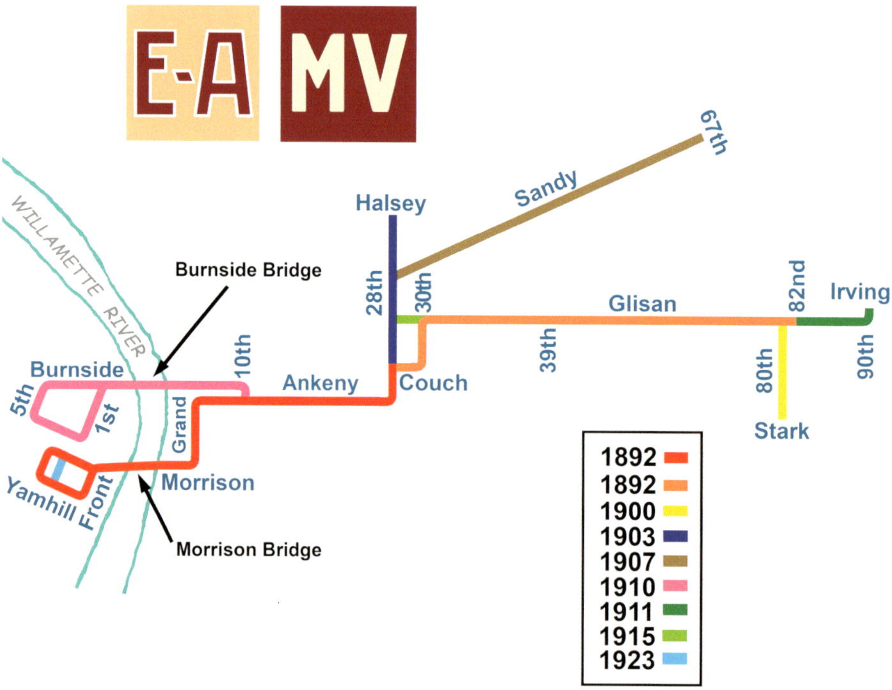

The City & Suburban Railway opened the East Ankeny Line to NE 28th and Couch streets in 1892, the same year they built an extension on NE Glisan Street. By 1900 the line had been relocated to SE 80th and Stark and renamed Montavilla. Extensions were added on East 28th Street in 1903 and Sandy Road in 1907. A final branch reached NE 90th and Irving in 1911. The ride to Montavilla was approximately 10 miles.

Inbound East Ankeny Line car 324 has turned onto Grand Avenue from Ankeny Street, closely followed by Russell-Shaver Line trolley 126. Prior to the establishment of the Bridge Transfer Line in 1915 passengers relied on R-S cars to connect with lines crossing the Willamette. The car has a full load, and it has been raining, but the conductor smiles for the camera. The date is around 1909.

Fuller No. 327 is seen at the northern terminus of the East Ankeny Line on NE Sandy Road. The road lives up to its name and the area is not yet developed in this 1911 view, but the coming of the streetcar will soon change things, as attested to by the dash sign referring to the new tracts of "Rose City Park, Rossmere and Hyde Park." (*Courtesy Mark Moore*)

SCENE OF THE MURDER OF CONDUCTOR C. L. NEVIUS BY A HIGHWAYMAN AND PHOTOGRAPH OF THE MURDERED MAN.

Conductor C. L. Nevius was murdered by highwaymen during a holdup that took place in 1907 after East Ankeny Line trolley No. 134 stopped at the Oregon Railroad & Navigation crossing on NE 37th Avenue and Sandy Road. The streetcar posed for this newspaper photograph is a City & Suburban "Standard," like car 134, and the conductor is standing in the door, as Nevius had been when attacked.

An East Ankeny Line "Summer Car" is crossing the second Morrison Street Bridge in this illustration from the 1912 guidebook *How to See Portland by Trolley*. There have been three Morrison bridges: the first was a wooden swing span that opened in 1887, and the second was another swing span that was built in 1905. The current bridge opened in 1958 and never carried streetcars.

East Ankeny Line car 456 was one of fifteen "Torontos" built at the Savier Street carbarn in 1902. They were the City & Suburban Railway's response to the rival Portland Railway Company's Fuller cars. It is seen at the E-A terminus on Sandy Road near present day NE 67th Street around 1907. Note the newspaper boy who has stopped to pick up his load of papers for delivery. (Note: colorization by the author.)

Mt. Tabor Villa Line car 71 presents a splash of white and gold colors as it traverses the Ladd Farm on NE Glisan Street during the autumn of 1892. On the left is the William S. Ladd residence and to the right his dairy barn sits where All Saints Church is today on NE 39th Avenue. The City & Suburban Railway had recently taken delivery of the brightly decorated Pullman trolley. (Note: colorization by the author.)

A Montavilla Line trolley is passing the Laurelhurst home now owned by Charles K. Henry in 1909, the year William S. Ladd's son William M. sold the Ladd Farm to the Laurelhurst Company. The streetcar is a first-series Fuller "Standard" built in 1902 by adding extended platforms and another set of wheels to an old single-truck trolley. The photograph is from a Laurelhurst Company brochure.

When this photograph was taken in 1907 students could ride trolleys to school. Those attending North Central High School were served by the East Ankeny Line. The charming 1890s building seen here, long since demolished, was located on the block bounded by East Burnside, NE 12th, Couch, and 13th Streets.

This picture of City & Suburban "Standard" 103 was taken at the Montavilla Line terminus on SE 80th and Glisan Streets. It was taken around 1900, when this trolley and the branch to Montavilla were new. The rollsign reads "MONTA.VILLA" but soon both the line and the community would be known by the single word contraction of Mt. Tabor Villa. Note the dispatcher's call box on the pole at right.

Jack Frost has visited NE 80th Avenue and Glisan Street in this *c.* 1915 photograph. Fowler's Drug Store and Wallace Grocery can be seen on the right and Engele's Shoe Repair and the Oddfellows Hall on the left. Hamilton's Funeral Parlor was on the ground floor of the Oddfellows building. In the distance, a 521-class PAYE car is heading towards the camera.

It took more than passenger cars to operate a street railway as seen here on February 13, 1916. Locomotive No. 911 is helping clear snow from the Montavilla Line on NE Glisan Street near 39th Street in Laurelhurst. A plow has been attached to Portland Railway, Light & Power's only narrow-gauge freight motor. It was of a type known as a "steeplecab" because of the sloping hoods. (Note: colorization by the author.)

While one branch of the Montavilla Line ran out NE Glisan Street to 90th, a second terminal was on SE 80th and Stark Streets, where we see PAYE car 595 around 1912. The dash sign "No Stops WEST of 29th St.," meant this was a limited. Traffic west of 29th was left to East Ankeny Line cars. (*Courtesy Clark County Historical Museum*)

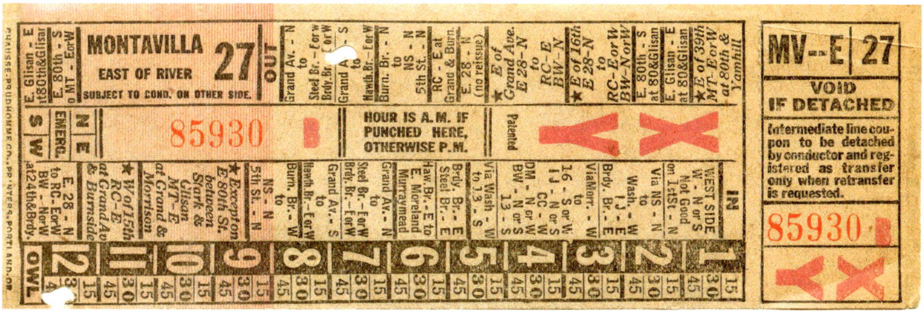

This Montavilla Line transfer is from the 1920s, when transfers were complicated. It is an MV–E transfer for use "east of the (Willamette) river" and was punched on a southbound trolley on Grand Avenue just before 1 a.m. Conditions on the back stipulate that it is for continuous travel in the same general direction. On the back it bears the name of Portland Electric Power Company First Vice President Franklin I. Fuller.

Four passengers and the motorman were injured on May 2, 1945, when Montavilla streetcar 471 crashed into a truck loaded with 5 tons of pipe at the corner of SE Washington Street and Grand Avenue. No one was injured, but motorman Walter Wolfe was cited. The demolished vestibule on unlucky No. 471 was rebuilt and the car returned to service where it suffered additional accidents.

No. 467 is travelling east through Laurelhurst on NE Glisan Street on its way to the terminus on SE 80th Avenue and Stark Street in Montavilla. It was one of the first group of PAYE cars ordered from the American Car Company in 1908. The twenty cars in this class featured squarish-looking bay window ends. By the late 1920s, destination signs included "Stark" or "90" to indicate the alternating terminals.

Plenty of 1940s advertising can be seen in this view of tired-looking Montavilla car 475 turning onto rain-soaked SE Grand Avenue from Morrison Street. On the roof of the Potter Drug Store at right are billboards for Heinz Mustard "He-Man Sandwiches" and Schlitz Beer and on the dash is an advertisement for Betsy Ross Bread.

The Montavilla streetcar line connected with Portland Railway, Light & Power Company's Mt. Hood Division station at what is now NE 90th Avenue and Irving Street. One of the 430-class trolleys can be seen here at the depot during the 1910s. From this terminal interurban trains left for Ruby Junction, Troutdale, Gresham, Bull Run, and way points until abandonment in 1927.

Kenn Lantz took this photograph of car 468 at the end of the line on NE 90th off Glisan Street as the last day for Montavilla streetcars loomed. The colors have faded on his original slide, yet they are still evocative of that warm summer of 1948. My friend and longtime railfan passed away in 2022 but his traction memories live on in scenes like this.

5
The Woodlawn Line

The Woodlawn Line was the fifth trolley operation to build through Northeast Portland. It utilized most of the route established by the Portland & Vancouver Railway in 1888 for its steam motor line but terminated in the community of Woodlawn, located on NE Dekum Street two blocks east of Union Avenue (now MLK Boulevard). Dekum Street was named for prominent merchant, banker and real estate investor Frank Dekum, who had helped finance the railway.

Woodlawn, although part of the City of Portland, resembled a small town with drugstores, groceries, meat markets, and restaurants, clustered around a little park containing a streetcar waiting room. Across the street from the ornate depot stood the Woodlawn Carbarn and yard that had originally served the little steam dummy trains. Residential tracts and churches spread out from the town center. A public school was built on nearby Union Avenue.

Woodlawn's streetcar commercial district obviated the necessity for frequent trips to Portland. However, the Commercial Club boasted three nearby trolley lines, providing local residents with quick service downtown when desired. A 1911 guidebook lists streetcars on the Vancouver, Woodlawn, and Union Avenue lines leaving at ten-minute intervals. The Union Avenue Line was a short-turn Alberta Line "tripper" providing local service during rush hours.

Portland & Vancouver Railway Company successor Portland Railway opened the Woodlawn Line in 1900. Woodlawn Line cars crossed into Portland via the Burnside Bridge, as had P&V trolleys after electrification in 1892. The other end of the line travelled over private right-of-way to a terminus at NE 8th and Dekum streets until 1911.

Tracks were steadily extended eastward along NE Dekum Street, with a final terminus established at NE 24th Street in 1914. Street paving did not keep pace, however, having reached no farther than 18th Street by 1924.

Streetcars assigned to the Woodlawn Line originally consisted of low-numbered trolleys like the Vancouver 40s, the 80-series open cars, and the first Fullers. When the Portland Railway Light & Power Company took over in 1906 400-class cars began to appear. After 1910, these were augmented with larger 521-class PAYEs.

The Woodlawn streetcar line was discontinued on February 20, 1937. It was replaced by a new Williams Avenue trolley bus line, which replaced the Williams Avenue streetcar line on the same date, February 21, and terminated at NE 18th Avenue and Dekum Street. This, in turn, bowed out to motor buses on February 17, 1952.

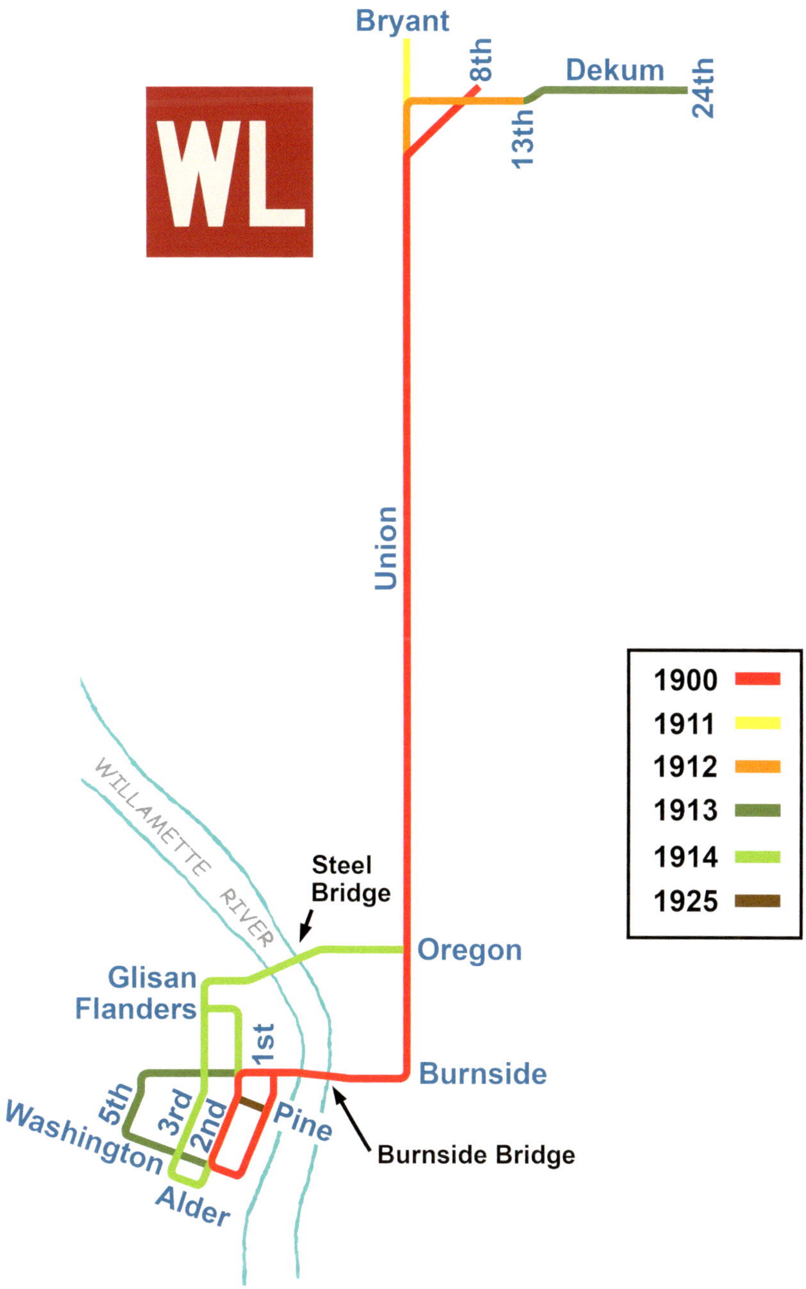

The Portland Railway Company opened the Woodlawn Line in 1900, using part of the route to Vancouver built by the Portland & Vancouver Railway for its 1888 steam "motor" operation. Portland Railway, Light & Power extended the line on NE Dekum to 24th Street in 1913. The eastside terminus remained here until 1937, while the westside terminals in downtown Portland changed to use various loops and, at different times over the years, two bridges. Length was approximately 8 miles.

This busy scene looks across the Portland & Vancouver Railway yard in Woodlawn. Two trains are in view, including a steam motor and two coaches on yard tracks and another engine and three coaches on the mainline. The view dates from June 1, 1890, two years before electrification, and construction is underway in an area that would become NE Madrona Street near Dekum.

Above left: Several interesting details can be seen in this *c.* 1905 view in Woodlawn. Three carmen are gathered around single truck open car 84. One leans against the railing in front of the depot, one is watching from Madrona Street and a third sits on the roof! In the background are the sand house, water tower, and the four-bay Woodlawn Carbarn. (*Courtesy Don Nelson*)

Above right: Portland Railway Woodlawn Line car 82 derailed on the east end of the Burnside Bridge on June 21, 1903, when the motorman braked to avoid falling through the draw, which had begun to open for a tow boat. Two women passengers suffered minor injuries, but it could have been much worse. If the open-air car had not hit an electrical pole, it would have fallen into the Willamette River.

Portland Railway No. 45 is in front of the Woodlawn Carbarn. A snow sweeper and freight car are on the right and at left is Portland & Suburban Express box motor 955. The express company provided freight and sprinkler service. Two-truck Brills like 45 proved too large for downtown use so were transferred here soon after arriving in 1892. Note the child next to the car and the notch cut into the barn for the trolley wire.

This Woodlawn Carbarn track plan is based on Sanborn's 1908 fire insurance map. The Portland & Vancouver Railway line can be seen cutting diagonally through town on Madrona Street. Ladder tracks cross in front of the water tower (blue circle) and into the barn. Behind the carbarn is an ice company. Across the street is a hotel. The depot is in the triangular block next to the brick building indicated in red.

This portrait of sixty-one "streetcar boys" appears to show the entire cadre of carmen assigned to the Portland Railway Company's Woodlawn Division. Details are mostly hidden in the 1902 image, but it is clear that the trolleys represent early rolling stock, including an 85-class open car and at least one of the first series Fuller "Standards." Note the lack of rollsigns. (*Courtesy Portland Archives*)

Carmen are posing with No. 331 in the yard in Woodlawn. The year is *c.* 1902, and the shiny Fuller streetcar is brand new and still lacking a rollsign. In the right background is the wood-frame Woodlawn Carbarn and behind the car is the large water tower left over from the Portland & Vancouver Railway steam dummy days. Its square walls were still in place at this time.

Three carmen are seen alongside car 331 in the Woodlawn yard so it may be part of a two-car train. The photograph was taken after the formation of the Portland Railway, Light & Power Company in 1906 since Portland Railway Company lettering has been removed. The wall around the water tower is also gone. Note the Fuller-type handbrakes visible through the front window.

Portland Consolidated Railway Company Woodlawn car 334 is waiting for passengers on NE Madrona Street near 7th Street *c.* 1904. It is a sunny day, and the windows are down in the smoking sections of the car. The ornate depot barely in view at far right was built by the Portland & Vancouver Railway Company in 1888. Note the color scheme looks lighter. (*Courtesy Mark Moore*)

Two 300-series Fuller streetcars are seen passing each other on SW Washington Street at the intersection with 4th Street in downtown Portland. The trolley closest to the camera in this 1909 postcard is on the Woodlawn Line. The ornate Victorian building housing the drugstore at center is long gone, but the Dekum Building behind it survives today.

The crews of two trolleys are having their picture taken with Woodlawn Line car 409 in this *c.* 1912 scene. Location is uncertain but since double track is in view this is either on NE Union and Bryant or on the Fern Street passing track near the new terminus on NE Dekum at 13th Street. No. 409 was built by the American Car Company in 1907 and was equipped with multiple-unit control.

Not a house is in sight as car No. 431 and crew lay over at the new Woodlawn Line terminus on NE 24th Street. The year is around 1913, because the Nelson Safety Fender now mandated by city ordinance is installed. The dash sign is now WL. The advertisement promoting the Gresham Chautauqua means it is spring. A sidewalk is in place, but the dirt road will remain for another decade. (*Courtesy Mark Moore*)

Conductor Adolph Schwarz and motorman Thomas West are in charge of car 470 in a picture taken at the Woodlawn Line terminal on NE Dekum and 24th Street around 1913. Both the trolley and neighborhood are largely empty in this early morning scene, yet building is underway as evidenced by the new craftsman style home at right. In the years before trolley retrievers, ropes were tied to cleats on the dash.

Conductor Welbury Walker and Motorman "Jos" Racer are pictured with car 472 at the eastern end of the Woodlawn Line during the early 1910s. The slight grades on Dekum Street presented little challenge to the twenty PAYE trolleys in this class, but in 1923, the series was upgraded with two additional GE-58 motors and reclassified as class "L" four-motor cars.

Posing with Woodlawn Line car 484 in this view on NE 24th and Dekum Streets are conductor Albert Porter and motorman Maurice Thompson. Like other end-of-the-line pictures, this was an official photograph taken for the employee record book kept at the Piedmont Carbarn on N Killingsworth Street. By the time this image was taken, the Woodlawn Carbarn was only used for storage.

Motorman Daniel Brown is smiling at the cameraman from the platform of car 571 yet conductor Edgar Hudson, with hands on hips, may be a bit impatient to go. On this warm, sunny day, two windows are open (with blinds pulled partially down) and the passenger boarding at rear has taken off his jacket. A modern-looking handbag is slung over his shoulder.

Car 575 was new when this picture was taken at the end of the Woodlawn Line on NE Dekum and 24th Streets. It was built in 1910 as part a group of 144 streetcars, the largest car order placed with the American Car Company in St. Louis. Behind Conductor Carl Schimelfenig and motorman Richard James, construction of new homes has begun.

Woodlawn car 579 is seen at the corner of NE Union Avenue and Alberta Street following a 1920s derailment. This minor event caused no damage, although it did attract a lot of attention, particularly from the kids clambering over the platform steps. The dash sign announces the opening of Oaks Amusement Park. In the background is the Walnut Park Theater. A Red Crown gas station is out of view at right.

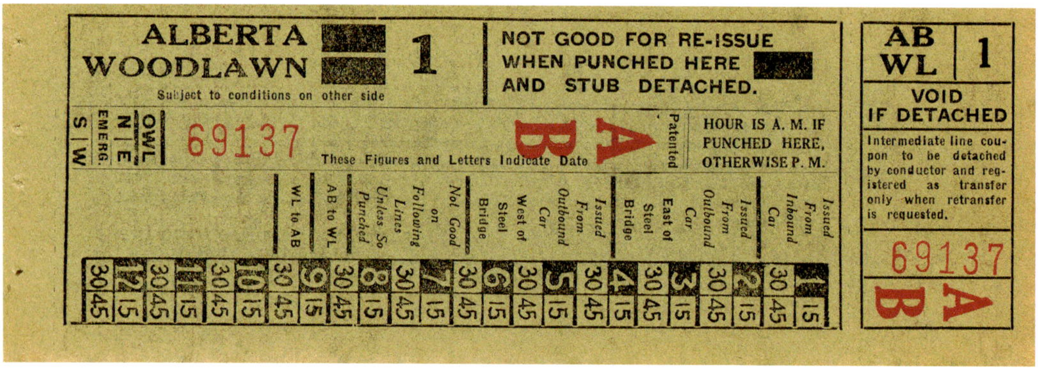

This unused 1930s Portland Traction Company transfer is for both the Alberta and Woodlawn lines. Possibly prompted by Great Depression cost-cutting, it reflects the similarity of much of these routes which both travelled across the Steel Bridge and along NE Union Avenue. Portland Traction Company Vice President W. H. Lines name appears on back.

6
The Alberta Line

The Alberta Line was opened on July 19, 1903, by the Portland Railway Company. During the first years, the route was also known as the Vernon Line after the neighborhood through which it ran. In 1906, it became part of the giant Portland Railway, Light & Power Company, which built a five-block eastward extension to 30th Street in 1908. The following year, the Alberta Line was extended to its final east side terminus at present-day NE 30th and Ainsworth Street. After that the route remained basically the same except during the reconstruction of the Steel Bridge.

Most changes to the Alberta Line involved terminals in downtown Portland, which were altered in response to bridge closures or track reconstruction. Various loops were tried, with routes varying between SW Washington, Alder, or Pine Streets.

Construction of double track or paving also caused changes in Northeast Portland. For example, in June 1926, a temporary bus shuttle began operating on NE 30th Street between Alberta and Ainsworth streets during track reconstruction.

In November 1908, a short-line service commenced on a portion of both the Alberta and Woodlawn lines. These "trippers" carried destination signs for Union Avenue and operated from downtown SW 2nd and Washington Street to Union Avenue and Alberta Street during evening rush hour. The service was discontinued in 1914.

Over the years, Alberta Line trolleys saw other changes. In 1909, nonstop limited operation was established on Union Avenue during evening rush hour, with local service relegated to the slower Union Avenue trippers. On February 13, 1911, two-car trains began operating on the line. Late night "owl service" was implemented in 1912. September 1, 1926, saw the introduction of one-man operation after the afternoon peak and on Sundays. During World War II, a "Designated Stop Plan" was carried out as a wartime economy effort whereby travel time was reduced and capacity increased by skipping certain stops.

During the PRL&P years, the maximum number of cars required to maintain schedules on the Alberta Line doubled from ten to twenty. The type of equipment assigned to the line also changed. In the early years, C&S "Standards" and Portland Railway Fullers were the norm. During the 1910s, the cars most often seen on the Alberta run were the 400–439 series multiple-unit cars, usually running in pairs. By the 1920s, the 400s had been joined by the 521-class PAYE cars. A few Broadway streamliners appeared in the last years. Alberta Line streetcars ceased operating on July 31, 1948. They were replaced by gasoline buses on August 1, 1948.

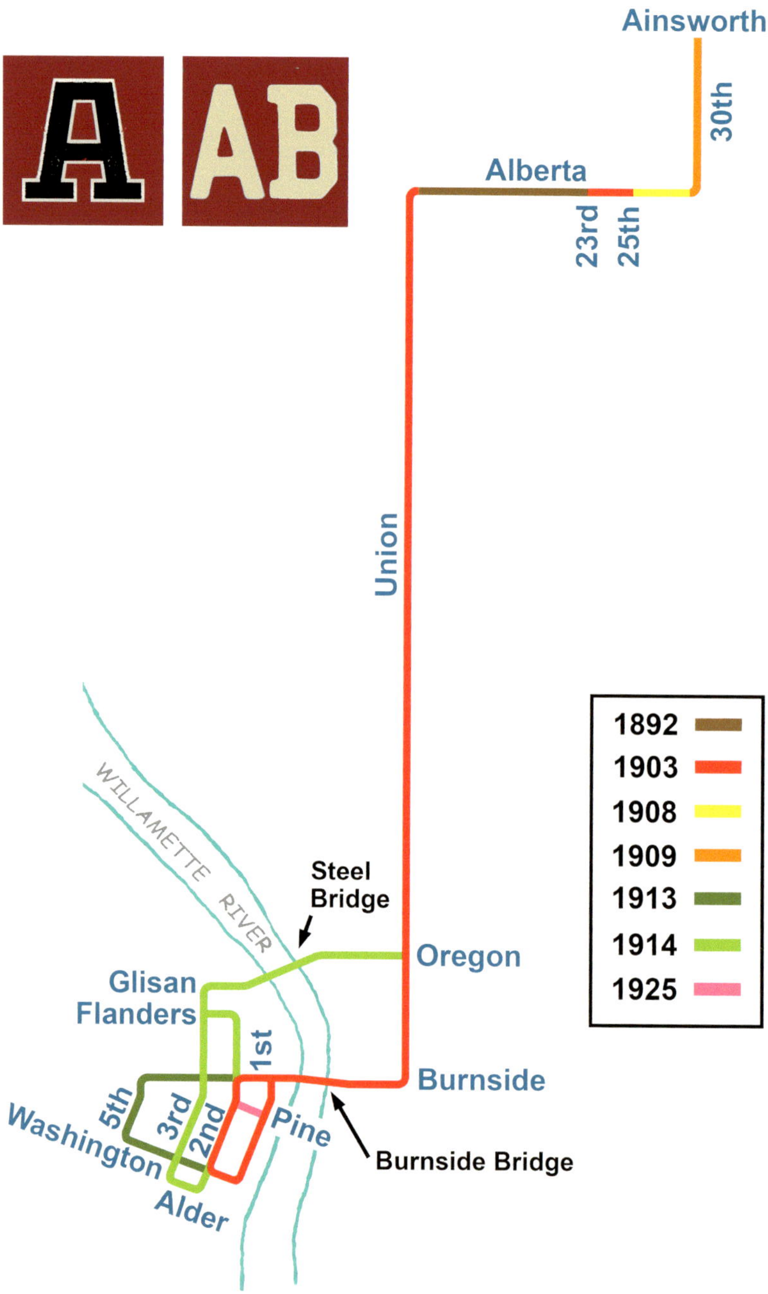

The Portland & Vancouver Railway Company began construction of the future Alberta Line with a branch from Union Avenue (now MLK) to NE 23rd in 1892. The final eastside terminus at NE 30th and Ainsworth came in 1909. A number of different downtown loops were used during the 1910s and '20s. The line was a little over 6 miles in length.

Construction of homes in the Vernon neighborhood referred to on the dash sign is just getting started in a photograph taken at what must be the NE 25th Avenue terminus of the Alberta Line. The location, plus cap badges, and lack of a rollsign, retriever, or permanent headlight, date the picture to before 1902. No. 84 was one of the Portland Railway open, single-truck, cars retired by 1908. (*Courtesy Don Nelson*)

No. 43 was one of six cars built by Brill in 1892 for the Multnomah Street Railway. Renumbered 93 by PRL&P, it is seen here signed for Union Avenue tripper duty after having been transferred to the Woodlawn Division. The double-truck cars were intended for Washington Street service, but management felt they were too large for use in downtown Portland. Note the safety gates.

Portland's most unique streetcar was assigned to the Alberta Line in 1914. The articulated trolley was created in 1913 by removing platforms from two old cars and hanging a conductor's cab between them. Capacity increased but students and others sometimes opened windows so friends could board without paying. Carmen James Price, Richard Taylor, and Paul Emanuelson are at the Ainsworth terminus.

This interior view of car 100–101 gives an idea of its size. The three sections were 73 feet in length overall and could accommodate 102 passengers including standees. Although the plan had been to build four such vehicles, and thus reduce the number of cars needed during rush hour, the experiment proved unsuccessful due to slow boarding and acceleration. No more were produced. (*Courtesy Mark Moore*)

Judging by the number of students who turned out to have their picture taken in front of Highland School, it must have been one of the largest grammar schools in Portland in 1907. The school, located on NE Wygant Street between 6th and 7th, was served by both Alberta and Woodlawn line streetcars.

Motorman August "Orie" Biddle and his conductor make ready to depart from the new Alberta Line terminus on NE 30th and Ainsworth with a group of fancily dressed passengers. Although they do not appear excited, two boys will be sitting in the front. The 1903 vintage open "breezer" is still lettered for the Portland Railway Company. It would be retired in 1917. (*Courtesy Mark Moore*)

Second-series Fuller No. 334 is thought to be at the original terminal on Alberta and 25th Streets in a picture taken around 1905. In the early days, smoking was allowed on the extended platforms at each end of the Fuller cars. The dash sign reads "take cars at Third and Yamhill for THE OAKS." Oaks Park opened in 1905, just before the Lewis & Clark Exposition. (Note: colorization by the author.)

Businesses of all kinds proliferate in this *c.* 1913 view of Alberta car No. 314 southbound on NE Union Avenue (now MLK) at Russell Street. On the left are a market, a pub, Russell Drug, Dentist Earl Muck, and a dance hall, and on the right are the Earlton Apartments, a tailor shop, a nickelodeon, a magazine store, a realtor, and an Excelsior Autocycle dealer. (Note: colorization by the author.)

Fuller No. 337 is seen with two unidentified carmen at the eastside Alberta Line terminus on Alberta Street sometime after Nelson Safety fenders were mandated by a 1912 city ordinance. PRL&P renumbered the car from Portland Railway No. 137 in 1906, but the fancy pinstriping remained until a later repainting. Note the planked boarding area in the dirt street.

This photograph at the final eastern terminus of the Alberta Line on 30th and Ainsworth Streets was taken in 1915, the year Thomas Ince's film *Civilization* was released. A dash sign promotes the showing of that movie at Oaks Park. It was a silent film portraying the horror of submarine warfare. Behind car 418, Edward Thompson's Piedmont Realty sells residential tracts. Note the AB sign. (*Courtesy Mark Moore*)

A flock of passengers have gathered with the crew of Alberta trolleys 422 and 421 to have their pictures taken on a hot day around 1910. The receptacles clearly seen next to the headlight are for multiple-unit control, which allowed the 400-series cars to operate in tandem with a single motorman and two conductors. Note the boy wearing baggy knickerbockers and long stockings. (*Courtesy Mark Moore*)

No. 431 and a sister are in front of the ladder tracks leading into the Piedmont Carbarn on N Killingsworth Street *c.* 1913. A three-man crew, including motorman Noah Stout and conductors Glen Saxton and Peter Bonneau, are in charge of a rush-hour tripper. The rollsign on the rear car says "Union Ave." and the train card in 431's window reads "tripper 5." A dash sign advertises skating at Oaks Park.

A child looks on as Conductor Dimmitt attempts to remove snow in front of car 549 while Motorman Columbia Cross clears the center window in a scene taken during the Silver Frost of January 1916. The location is thought to be near the northern terminus of the Alberta Line on NE 30th Street. In those days crews were required to stay with vehicles stranded by a storm. (Note: colorization by the author.)

Telegrams were delivered by streetcar in 1919. This one from Boston, MA, was sent, via the Postal Telegraph & Cable Company's Special Rush Service, to Mrs. W. J. Frost on E 9th Street N (changed to NE 9th in 1933). Penciled-in notations indicate it would be delivered via the "Alberta Car" to a home five blocks "off Skidmore" Street.

PAYE car 567 is brand new in this *c.* 1911 picture at the end of the Alberta Line. Conductor Marion Hall and motorman John Lentz also look young. Lentz is leaning against the car and holding the controller handle in a gloved hand. The street is unpaved, but at least there are lights above the terminus. The sign in the background advertises Tate Investment Company lots for sale.

Alberta car 584 is passing through the Vernon commercial district at NE 17th and Alberta Streets. Establishments seen in this *c.* 1910 postcard include on the right, Vernon Drug, Peterson & Jackson Grocery, Vernon Social Club, Ford's Pool Hall and Lunch Counter, H. B. Garrison Dentist, and Dr. Smith Surgeon. Storefronts at left include Halliday's Confectionary, a jeweler, a shoe store, and a realtor.

Buildings in view in this 1930 scene showing Alberta Line trolley 418 crossing the intersection of W Burnside and 3rd Avenue include, from left to right: the Union Theater, Union Café, Lind Hotel, Worcester Building, Multnomah Hotel, Winchester House Hotel, Tacoma Brew, and Union Clothing. Within two years, the Victorian-style Worcester Building and the old Winchester House would be gone.

The operator of Alberta car 400 holds a long metal switch iron as he leans out the window to turn the switch on SW 3rd Avenue and Washington Street on March 1, 1936. In June 1914, as the commercial center of town began shifting to the west, 3rd Street reinvented itself by installing lighted archways over each intersection between Yamhill and Burnside. The last arches were removed in 1940.

The evening shadows are growing as Alberta trolley 402 leans into the curve on the corner of NE Alberta Street and Union Avenue. The car is an evening tripper heading back to the carhouse on N Killingsworth Street. On the dash is a 1940s advertisement for Hedda Hopper's Hollywood gossip column in *The Journal*. The building at right survives today.

Alberta Line cars 406 and 413 are seen meeting on the passing track on NE 30th Avenue and Killingsworth Street during the 1940s. The house at right and the commercial buildings in the background still exist today. These streetcars were a bit faster following the addition of two more motors in 1923. However, they remained a softly sprung, rough riding class. This pair were retired in 1948.

No. 406 is at the Alberta Line terminus in a 1944 picture looking northward on wet NE 30th Avenue. Things look peaceful, but in April 1934 two masked men held up operator Robert Simmons here at gun point, taking his coin changer and $10 in cash. Only the white building in the right background remains today. At left is a Buy Rite Grocery panel truck. *(Courtesy City of Portland Archives)*

Inbound Alberta car 408 is coming down the west approach to the Steel Bridge about 1948, followed closely by Broadway No. 814 working its namesake line. The sign on the right reads, "SLIPPERY WHEN WET OR FROSTY." The dash advertisement on No. 408 is for Crown Flour, a product of Crown Mills in Northwest Portland, one of the largest producers of flour in the Pacific Northwest.

Alberta streetcars 423 and 417 are turning from NE Alberta Street onto Union Avenue during the 1940s. Piedmont Hardware, on the corner, was a neighborhood landmark. It included a soda fountain and sold much more than hardware, as can be seen from the window displays. The building survives today. Note the signal on the sidewalk at right.

The tree-lined Concordia neighborhood forms a pleasant backdrop for this *c.* 1942 view of No. 427 changing ends at NE 30th and Ainsworth. A sign on the dash depicts Crown Flour as part of the WWII effort to maintain a healthy diet, exclaiming "Vitamins for Victory." Still wearing its 1930s green and cream colors, this trolley would be the first of its class to be retired in 1944.

A woman scurries in front of outbound Alberta trolley 429 on the corner of NE 30th Avenue and Killingsworth Street. Perhaps she has just bought groceries at George Ingram's 30th Avenue Store, where "spuds are five for 29 cents" and cucumbers are 15 cents each. The date is June 12, 1948, and Alberta Line streetcars will cease operating in two weeks. (*Charles Hayden photograph*)

A rainy post-WWII view of No. 804 at NE 30th Avenue and Ainsworth Street shows that Broadway type streamliners have now been added to the Alberta run. In 1932, the fifteen Broadway cars had been Portland's first new car order in nearly twenty years, and also its last. The dash sign is for the Billy Rose column in the *Oregon Journal*. (*Courtesy Wayne Roberts*)

Inbound Broadway type car 809 is seen crossing the Steel Bridge in 1948, the last year for Alberta Line operation. No. 809 has been freshly painted in the final Portland Traction Company red and cream color scheme, with V-shaped ends and diamond sides. One of these Brill Master Units is preserved today by the Oregon Electric Railway Historical Society in Brooks, Oregon. (*Robert McVay photograph*)

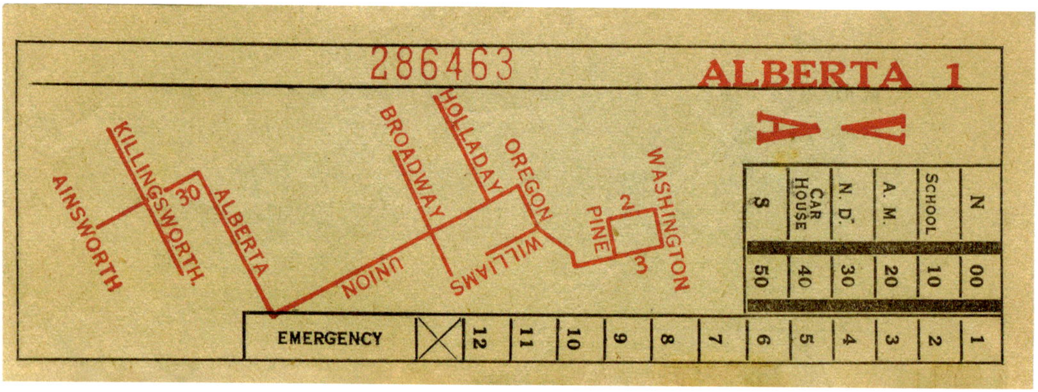

This unused Alberta Line transfer is of the modern type adopted in the 1930s. Operators would place a punch on the map to indicate the place a passenger boarded. The route illustrated on this transfer shows the Alberta Line as it was from 1925 onwards with cars crossing the Willamette River via the Steel Bridge. Listed on the back is Gordon G. Steele, who became Portland Traction Company's president in 1935.

7
The Broadway Line

The Broadway Line became what many would call Portland's most prestigious route, and the newest streetcars would be assigned to it. But it was not always that way. When the first Portland Railway Company inaugurated service on the line on November 23, 1903, it ran from downtown Washington Street to a nondescript area a few blocks north of Sullivan's Gulch. As of yet, there was no Broadway Bridge and SW Broadway was years away from being a trendy commercial district.

Until 1909, the eastside terminal for the Broadway Line was at what is now NE 21st and Halsey Streets. The tracks on Halsey were abandoned on September 28, 1909, when Portland Railway, Light & Power opened a new branch to NE 22nd and Thompson. Meanwhile, trippers were soon running farther east on a short extension on Broadway between NE 22nd and 24th Streets. It was built so that visiting U.S. President William Howard Taft could ride the streetcar to a cornerstone ceremony at the new Unitarian Universalist Church.

As lots sold out in booming Irvington real estate companies turned to land farther east in what would become the Alameda, Rose City Park and Beaumont neighborhoods. In 1910, realizing that streetcar lines were a pipeline to further development, the Alameda Land Company reimbursed PRL&P for operation of a shuttle service up the hill to Mason Street where dairy land and orchards were being cleared for the Alameda Park tract. The streetcar company had originally intended to loop back on 24th Street; however, in February 1911, they changed their mind and the shuttle was replaced. While short-lined trippers turned back at Fremont Street, streetcars in regular service began climbing Regents Drive to present day NE 29th and Mason streets.

The streetcar would usher in two kinds of growth. By 1912, the area once called Gravelly Hill was a fashionable streetcar suburb known as the Alameda. Meanwhile, Broadway, along the southern edge of the route, was developing into a commercial district. Throughout the 1920s, several residential properties there were converted into businesses. That process would accelerate after November 1930 when the street was widened and trees removed.

Over the years, Broadway Line streetcars utilized three different bridges to cross the Willamette River. During 1903–12, they reached downtown via the Burnside Bridge. On September 8, 1912, the crossing shifted to the new Steel Bridge. One year later, they moved to the new Broadway Bridge. Since it connected with NE Broadway, SW 7th Street was renamed Broadway and trolleys now operated along Broadway all the way from NE 24th to SW Jefferson. Except for repaving in 1916 and 1927, things stayed that way until 1940 when the route reverted to the Steel Bridge a final time. The only other significant change for the Broadway Line came during World War II when skip-stop service was established to reduce travel time and increase capacity, as it was on most other city lines.

One-man operation was first used on the Broadway Line after the evening rush hour and on Sundays starting on February 1, 1927. On May 17, 1932, all runs were assigned a single operator instead of the traditional crew consisting of a motorman and conductor. Another break in tradition came with the new Broadway type streetcars, which used Ohmer fare boxes instead of the clock-like fare registers mounted on bulkheads.

From 1903 until 1910, C&S "Standards" and Fuller cars were assigned to Broadway Line service. After 1910, large-vestibuled PAYE cars built by the American Car Company made their appearance. In 1932, the iconic 800 series debuted on the Broadway run. The most advanced cars ever to join the Portland Traction fleet were soon nicknamed "the Broadways" after the line they were most associated with. Local newspapers described these streamliners as "the last word in streetcars." Indeed, for Portland they would be.

At first, only six trolleys were required for peak operation on the Broadway Line. At other times of the day, three cars sufficed. The need for additional cars at rush hour increased steadily from eight in 1909, to nine in 1910, a dozen in 1911, and fifteen after 1912. The trend reversed during the 1920s. As ridership slowly dropped not as many streetcars were needed. On August 1, 1948, Broadway streetcars were replaced by 900-series gasoline buses.

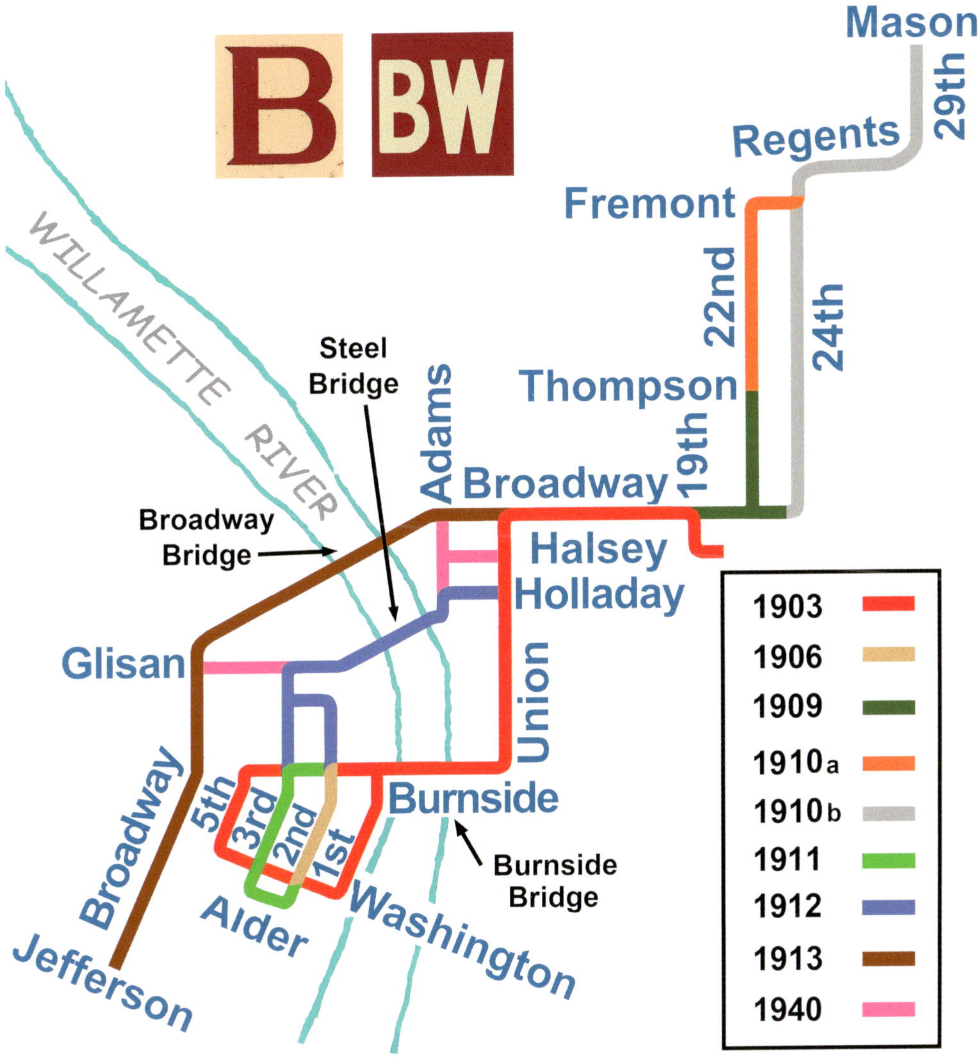

The Broadway Line originally ran across the Burnside Bridge from downtown to new developments along NE Halsey Street north of Sullivan's Gulch. In 1909 tracks were removed from Halsey and a new route built north into the Irvington neighborhood via NE 22nd Street. The extension to Fremont Street opened in 1909. In 1910, a shuttle car operated up the Regents Drive hill. By late 1910, the Alameda Park tract became the outer terminus for the regular line. Several downtown loops and three different bridges were used at different points in the line's history. The line length was nearly 7 miles.

Portland Consolidated Railway No. 339 is at the original eastside Broadway Line terminal on NE Halsey and 21st Streets in 1905. The second-series Fuller Standard car was built by the Portland Railway Company in 1901. It is seen waiting for passengers in a quiet residential setting. (*Courtesy Mark Moore*)

In 1912, Broadway Line streetcars crossed the Willamette River via the Steel Bridge and traversed the downtown commercial center on 3rd Street. This postcard of Fuller No. 310 was published before the Great Light Way arches were installed in 1914. Once a landmark, the tall Chamber of Commerce Building on the left was razed in 1934.

There is nothing but trees behind Fuller No. 340 to help identify its location; however, this may be at the new terminus on 29th and Mason Streets. One clue is the billboard at right, which advertises the Alameda Park Addition. The date is around 1911 and the lettering for the Portland Consolidated Railway Company has not yet been painted over. (*Courtesy Mark Moore*)

Both trolley 568 and the Mason Street terminus are new in this 1911 photograph. At that time the Alameda Land Company was subsidizing a temporary shuttle service between here and NE Fremont Street to help develop real estate. The carmen look reluctant to step into the quagmire on NE 29th Street.

The crew of Broadway Line car 570 is snowbound on NE 24th and Tillamook Streets about 1915. This location on the eastern edge of the Irvington neighborhood had been the terminus of the line for a few months in 1909 during construction of the loop track to NE Fremont. Note the dash-sign route designation is now two letters. (Note: colorization by the author.) (*Courtesy Jerry Risberg*)

The crew of Broadway Line car 573 is exhibiting interesting body language in this view looking southwest from the corner of NE 29th and Mason Streets around 1913. The conductor looks impatient, and the motorman appears to be suppressing a smile. The Alameda Land Company office is on the right and a classic "four square" house on the left. The home still stands today. (*Courtesy Mark Moore*)

Conductor Joseph Poppino and motorman "Otto" Ottosen are seen with PAYE type car 642 at the Mason Street Broadway Line terminus during the 1910s. This photograph looking north on a damp 29th Street shows a neighborhood still under development. The sign on the right side of the dash reads "UNION AND NORTH BANK DEPOTS," which this car went past or came close to.

NE Broadway looked much different before the street was widened in 1930 and the trees taken out. This view looks east from Union Avenue. Except for the State laundry and Gilmore Gasoline station at left, the area remains largely residential. Further change would come in 1932, when the streamlined new Broadway streetcars appeared. After that the PAYE car seen approaching here would be relegated to tripper service.

Southbound Broadway Line car 571 is about to pass a northbound Mississippi Avenue Line trolley in this 1929 picture looking southward on rain-swept SW Broadway from Oak Street. This was the theater district, and the Music Box, Orpheum, and Paramount can be seen on the right. Also at right is the Hotel Benson. All theaters but the Paramount are gone today.

A Willys Knight automobile trails exhaust smoke as it passes Broadway Line car 560 at the intersection of SW Broadway and W Burnside Street in 1929. The Hotel Scott at left is long gone, but the National Portland Garages building in the background survives today and is still a garage. First-floor retail included the General Steamship Corporation and Griffin's Cafeteria.

Here's Newest Thing in Streetcars – All for Portland

Franklin T. Griffith, president of the PEP Co., Friday placed an order with Philadelphia manufacturers for 15 new streetcars, representing an investment of $250,000 for use on local lines. Griffith is hopeful, he said, that the equipment will be here and read to go by May 1. Each of the new cars has a capacity of 41 passengers; are modern, one-man, automatic, front-entrance, rear-exit, cross-seat, drop-your-own-fare type -- quite the last word in street railway rolling stock.

When the Quaker Line steamship *San Clemente* docked in Portland harbor on April 30, 1932, it had on board cars 801 and 802, part of the first consignment of fifteen streetcars ordered by the Portland Traction Company from J. G. Brill in Philadelphia. At a cost of just over $12,000 apiece, they were the last new car order for Portland, which never purchased the famous PCC cars introduced in other cities.

Outbound and inbound Broadway cars 801 and 814 are seen in front of the Alameda Drugstore at the corner of NE 24th Avenue and Fremont Street during the 1940s. As with many, this corner pharmacy included a soda fountain, which made it a destination for neighborhood youth. The dash sign advertises the funny papers in the Sunday *Oregon Journal*.

This view looks in the opposite direction from the previous one as inbound Broadway car 802 turns onto NE 24th Avenue from Fremont Street during the 1940s. A small sign in the window above the operator reads "29th & Mason," which means this was a through trolley to the end of the line and not a tripper. Note that the Broadways did not use the traditional roof-mounted rollsigns.

Broadway car 802 is at the NE 29th Avenue and Mason Street terminus on July 2, 1948, shortly before the abandonment of the Broadway Line. The streamlined Brill Master Unit is resplendent in Portland Traction Company's red and cream livery, yet in two years the scrapper's torch awaits. (*Lawson Hill photograph, courtesy Morning Sun Books*)

Eastbound car 806 is at the front of a bevy of Broadways stuck in the snow on NE Broadway at Union Avenue on January 21, 1943. The Trading Post in the background was a used furniture store. To the left, a roof-mounted billboard heralds "The Coke's in" in a World War II advertisement depicting servicemen gathering around a waitress serving Coca-Cola. (Note: colorization by the author.)

You can almost hear the swishing sound of tires on rainy pavement as Broadway car 808 travels eastward along NE Broadway during the 1940s. The commercial buildings in the left background, including Nepom's Market on the corner of NE 6th Avenue, are still standing. However, the early twentieth-century homes have been replaced by vacant lots.

The rays of the sun glint off the side of Broadway car 809 as it rolls through rush-hour traffic on NE Broadway at 22nd Avenue in the late 1940s. The gas stations in the background are gone today but some of the large Craftsman-style houses survive. This was in the time when "service" stations really did provide driver assistance. The one on the left offers S&H Green Stamps and "charging while you wait."

Broadway car 810 is on N Williams Avenue approaching Broadway closely followed by Mack trolley coach No. 141. The old Victorian building in the background houses the Tom Benson Glass Company. On the right are the Savoy Apartments. The Williams Avenue trolley bus line outlasted the Broadway streetcar since it operated from February 21, 1937, until February 16, 1952.

No. 811 is laying over at the Broadway Line terminus during the late 1940s. The brick home on the corner of NE 29th Avenue and Mason Street is still there today. The bright red and cream livery in this scene was a later replacement for the gray, green, ivory, and black that these cars arrived with in 1932. The color layout on the car ends was later modified as shown in the picture below.

The interesting detail in this view of Broadway car 812 changing ends at the NE 29th Avenue terminus is the new Portland Traction Company logo on the side, which dates the photograph to 1948. The words near the door read "please have fare ready" and the two small signs at the top of the windshield are "29th and Mason" and (train) "2."

Broadway car 812 is eastbound on the west end of the Steel Bridge on June 10, 1948. The gas storage tank in the background is long gone, a casualty of the conversion to natural gas. At one time gas for heating and cooking was made by carbonizing coal. Known as "coal gas" or "town gas," it was barged up the river and stored in large containers like this.

Trolley 813 is heading west past the State laundry, and a corner drugstore, on NE Broadway at Grand Avenue. Upon retirement from city line service in 1950, this car was renumbered 4012, becoming one of two Broadways (the other was 800/4014) converted to standard gauge for use on the lines to Oregon City and Bellrose. Today it is at the Oregon Electric Railway Historical Society museum in Brooks, Oregon.

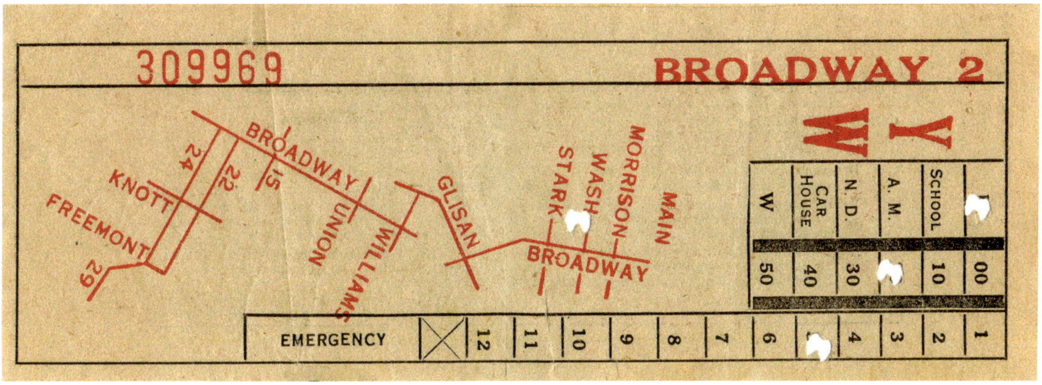

The passenger using this modern-style Portland Traction Company transfer boarded an outbound Broadway Line streetcar on downtown Washington Street at 5:20 p.m. during an evening rush hour in the early 1930s. Gordon G. Steele was still a Portland Traction Company's vice president at the time. Operators, and before them conductors, each had ticket punches with unique patterns.

After retirement in 1950, Broadway No. 809 was used to store a rockhound's collection in Aurora, Oregon. After he passed away in the 1970s, the car was hauled to the Trolley Park in Glenwood, Oregon where the center section was cut away. The shortened car, looking more like a Birney, now resides in an Old Spaghetti Factory restaurant in Sacramento, California. (*Photograph by the author*)

8
The Sandy Boulevard Lines

The last three streetcar lines to serve Northeast Portland were extensions, or stub lines, running out Sandy Road, which was renamed Boulevard after paving in 1913. All were built at the behest of real estate companies opening up Portland's largest new developments. The first of these was the Rose City Park Line, which was built by Hartman & Thompson realtors in 1907 and operated through an agreement with the Portland Railway, Light & Power Company. PRL&P would later take over all three lines.

The Rose City Park Line was an extension of the East Ankeny Line from NE 28th Street and Sandy Road to a terminus at 67th Street. Unlike its two stub line neighbors, Rose City Park ran through to downtown Portland. Its Southwest Portland terminals changed a few times over the years, from 2nd and Yamhill Streets in 1907, to 2nd and Washington in 1910, and 2nd and Alder in 1911. The Rose City Park Line was extended to NE 82nd Street in February 1912. By 1930, as more tracts were built, the Rose City Park designation had been shortened to simply the Rose City Line.

Next came the Beaumont Line, an on-again off-again stub built under an agreement with the Beaumont Land Company. It opened in December 1911 as a shuttle from the Rose City Park Line at NE 42nd Street and Sandy Road to NE 41st and Wistaria Drive in the Alameda neighborhood. In both the morning and evening rush hours, through service was provided to downtown 5th and Washington Streets. During the rest of the day, passengers had to transfer from the Rose City Park Line.

The Beaumont Line became a stub line only service on March 30, 1912, due to grading and resurfacing on Sandy Road and the installation of double tracks on the Rose City Park Line. By October 16, connection to Sandy Road had been restored and the line resumed operating downtown during rush hours. On April 1, 1914, Beamont cars began operating to 5th and Washington Streets all day except for the first hour in the morning and last hour in the evening. One-man operation was implemented at the same time.

Beaumont trolleys crossed the Willamette River via the Burnside Bridge until repair work in 1913–14 shifted them to the Morrison Bridge. A further route change onto the Steel Bridge took place during 1924–26 due to construction of the new Burnside Bridge.

The last streetcar line built in Northeast Portland was the Parkrose Line, which ran along the side of Sandy Road from the end of the Rose City Park Line at NE 82nd Street and Sandy Road to 122nd Street in Parkrose. This stub line was built and operated by the Portland & Troutdale Electric Company, which had been incorporated on November 7, 1911, by the Hartman & Thompson real estate company. Hartman & Thompson had moved their base of operations from the Rose City Park development to the small farming community of Parkrose where they established a fifty-home tract promoted as being, "right in the path of Portland's growth."

The P&T Electric inaugurated service on the 1.5-mile Parkrose Line on February 4, 1912, using two old cars leased from PRL&P. To differentiate them from others these trolleys were repainted in green with gray trim.

Equipment varied on the Sandy Boulevard lines. In warm weather open trolleys built by the City & Suburban Railway in 1903 might be seen on the Rose City Park Line; however, starting in 1909, most of the streetcars assigned to Rose City Park were the new 521-class PAYE cars built for PRL&P by the American Car Company. In contrast, older cars were used on the stub lines. The Beaumont Line began service with 1900-vintage C&S "Standard" trolleys. These proved adequate even after the line began running through to downtown; however, larger PAYE cars were also used at times. The neglected sister was, of course, the Parkrose Line, which had the oldest cars. The two outdated C&S cars were all that was needed for Parkrose duty. Occasionally small PRL&P trolleys could be spotted on the line while the C&S veterans were receiving maintenance service. Six or seven streetcars were adequate for Rose City and Beaumont line operation.

The first line in Northeast Portland to be abandoned was, predictably, the Parkrose run, which stopped in October 1928. The Beaumont Line soldiered on until September 2, 1936, after which it was replaced by a longer bus line. The Rose City Line lasted longer, ceasing on November 28, 1936. It was replaced by the Sandy Boulevard trolley bus, which gave way to regular motor buses on October 23, 1958.

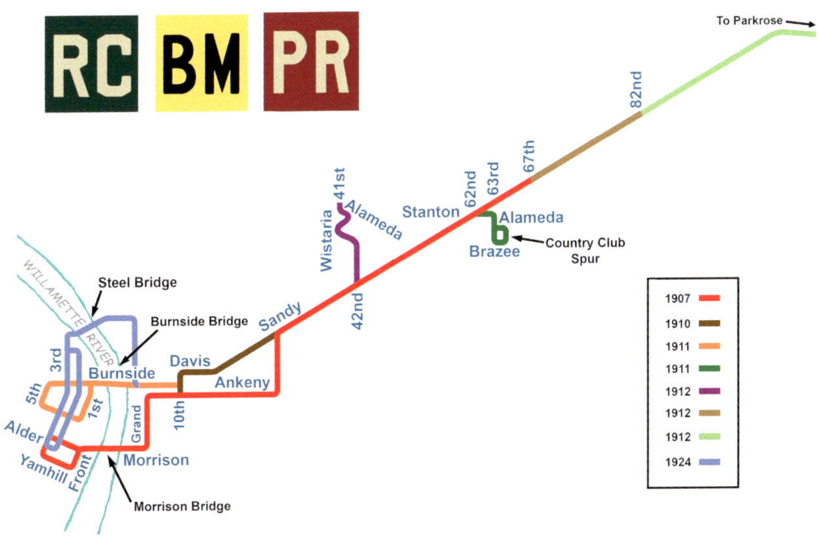

The Rose City Park Line began running from downtown in 1907. The Beaumont Line opened in March 1912. Last was the Parkrose Line, which reached 122nd and Sandy in October 1912.

These East Ankeny Line trippers are on Rose City Park Line tracks at Sandy Road and Coleman Avenue (now NE 62nd Avenue). They are waiting to pick up passengers from the old Portland Country Club and Livestock Association racetrack. Around 1908, a spur was built from here to the club grounds so traffic would not be held up on the mainline.

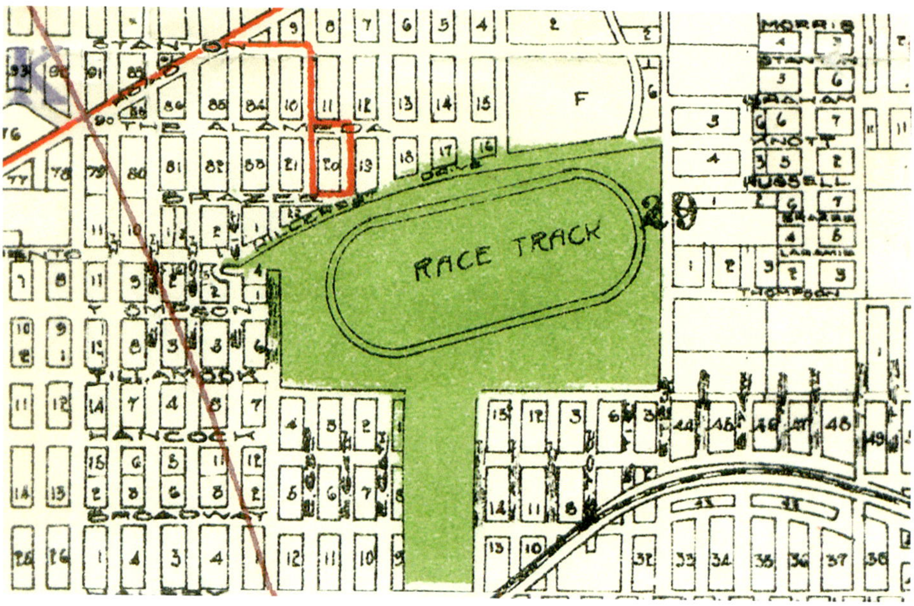

This detail from the American Map and Reproducing Company's 1912 Map of Portland and Vicinity shows the half-mile spur running from 62nd Street and Sandy Road to a loop at the racetrack on Brazee Street. In December 1917 PRL&P successfully petitioned the City Council for permission to abandon the lightly used line in order to avoid required maintenance. By 1919, it had disappeared from maps.

A speedster raises clouds of dust as it whips around the one-mile dirt track renamed the Rose City Speedway in 1910 by landowner Fred T. Merrill, who sought to promote Portland as a major horse, motorcycle, and auto racing venue. The site included a covered grandstand, horse barns, and exhibition buildings. Soon after the racetrack closed in 1921, it was replaced with today's Rose City Golf Course.

Brand-new trolley 561 is thought to be at the earlier Rose City Park Line terminus on Sandy Road at 67th Street during a sunny day in 1910. PRL&P lumped together three nearly identical car series from the American Car Company in St. Louis to form Portland's largest class. Cars 521–560 were built in 1909, numbers 561–600 came in 1910, and 601–665 in 1911.

Construction is evident as new PAYE streetcar 540 climbs up the hill on NE Sandy Road around 1911. Customers are lining up in front of the Hubbell and Son real estate office on the corner of 52nd Street on the right, and a new pump house is being built on the hill above. The line served the new Rosemere, Rose City Park, Merlow, and Belle Crest tracts. (*Courtesy Mark Moore*)

Rose City Park Line car 556 is seen at the NE 82nd Street and Sandy Road terminus in 1912. The dash sign in the early years included the new Rosemere and Beaumont tracts. The shelter for Parkrose passengers is already in place, sitting in front of vacant lots. No. 556 was less than two years old when this photograph was taken.

No. 216 waits at the end of the Rose City Park Line on NE Sandy Boulevard and 82nd during the summer of 1914. The waiting station for Parkrose passengers is behind the car. The dash advertisement is for an August Playground Festival at Columbia Park. Car 216 was one of twenty-five open breezers built by the City & Suburban Railway in 1903 and seldom used after 1919. (*Courtesy Mark Moore*)

Inbound and outbound Rose City Park cars 561 and 562 are seen meeting at 82nd Street and Sandy Boulevard in 1917. Dashboard advertisements, "Are You Pledged?" and "Hit the Liberty Trail," encourage riders to buy World War I Liberty Bonds. Note the motorman attired like a steam railroad locomotive engineer of the time. A lone Craftsman-style home can be seen at left.

The crew posing for their picture with car 564 at the Rose City Line terminus on NE Sandy Boulevard at 82nd Street seems unaware of the boy bouncing up and down on the newly installed Nelson Safety Fender at right. The dash sign, "SEE SIGNS ON POLES FOR SKIP STOPS" refers to the World War I conservation measure. Note another motorman decked out in "motoneer" garb.

Rose City Park streetcar 608 is crossing a temporary trestle over the Oregon-Washington Railroad & Navigation Company tracks at 37th Street and Sandy Boulevard. Prior to the regrade project, the OWR&N had operated through Sullivan's Gulch at grade. This was the first of seven viaducts constructed over depressed railroad right-of-way during 1916–18 to eliminate dangerous crossings.

Inbound Rose City car 651 is on the west approach to the new Burnside Bridge. Burnside Street was widened in 1931 by removing several building fronts and adding a new lane. The second Burnside Bridge was completed on May 28, 1926, and originally included ornate concrete trolley poles and center-of-the-street boarding islands reached by a pedestrian underpass.

No. 657 is headed west through the Hollywood shopping district on Sandy Boulevard at NE 41st Avenue on April 12, 1934. An aproned grocer is handing change to a shopper on the sidewalk in front of the Sunny Jim Market at left. Businesses in view across the street include a drugstore, a market, the First National Bank and J. C. Penney.

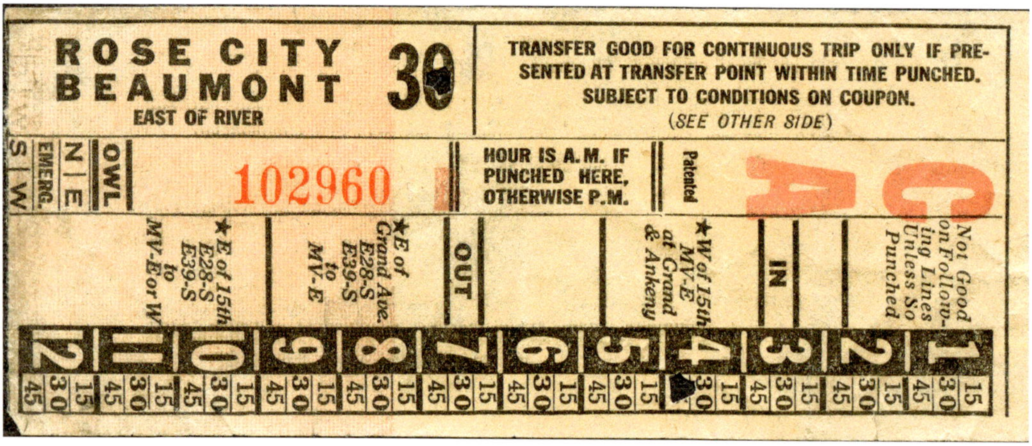

Like the Alberta and Woodlawn lines, the routes for Rose City and Beaumont were similar so a single transfer was used for both. This one was issued in the mid-1930s when W. H. Lines was vice president and general manager of the Portland Electric Power Company. It was punched on a Beaumont line car on the east side of the Willamette River at 4:45 p.m. during the afternoon rush hour.

Mack trolley bus No. 344, coming from the Ankeny Carbarn, is turning onto Sandy Boulevard from NE 28th Avenue to enter service in 1940. The Sandy Boulevard Line opened on November 30, 1936, and was converted to motor buses twice before being discontinued a final time on October 23, 1958. It was one of the last four trolley bus routes in Portland. Both of the buildings in this photograph are extant today.

A young passenger looks on as the crew readies trolley 143 for another trip on the Beaumont Line. The conductor has swept out the car and the motorman has removed the controller handle. The year is 1912, when most Beaumont cars provided a shuttle service from Sandy Road to The Alameda. Those Craftsman-style homes in the background at NE 42nd and Sandy are gone today. (Note: colorization by the author.)

In spite of appearances, this is not a two-car train. Beaumont Line trolley 555 and a Rose City Line car are trapped together in the snow on the old Burnside Bridge during what is thought to have been the Big Snow of 1916. There are three carmen because the Rose City trolley had a conductor and motorman, but the Beamont car was operated by one man. (Note: colorization by the author.)

Since 1914, the Beaumont Line had operated with one-man streetcars. But, as seen in this picture taken downtown in 1927, the Portland Electric Power Company used uniformed employees called "leaders" to help out during the afternoon rush hour. They speeded things up by collecting fares on the sidewalk and letting passengers into the rear vestibule of the car.

Fully loaded Beaumont car 129 is turning onto Union Avenue from Oregon Street during a September 1924 rush hour. It is about to pass inbound Rose City Park No. 473. Both trolleys have been rerouted to use the Steel Bridge during construction of the new Burnside Bridge, which would continue for two years. The arrow at center points to newsboy Larry Griffith, who would become a lifetime streetcar enthusiast.

Portland & Troutdale Electric Railway car 136 is about to overtake a "flivver" as it heads westward along the side of Sandy Boulevard during the 1920s. The veteran trolley was one of forty-seven "Standards" built by the City & Suburban Railway in 1900. It was leased from PRL&P for use on the Parkrose Line and painted green with gray trim.

The streetcar seen here in front of the Parkrose depot on NE Sandy Boulevard at 122nd Street was not regularly used on the line. No. 305 was a first-series Fuller car rebuilt with three compartments by the Portland Railway Company in 1902 from an old Pullman. It would have been a substitute for one of the 100-class cars while it was in the shop for maintenance. Note the East Ankeny rollsign and PRL&P colors.

9
Streetcars Return to Northeast Portland

The last three streetcar lines in Northeast Portland, Alberta, Broadway, and Montavilla, ceased operation on August 1, 1948, consigning sixty years of ringing steel and clanging bells to the realm of bygones. The Sandy Boulevard trolley bus lasted a decade longer, until October 23, 1958. After that, trolleys would be gone from the Rose City for nearly thirty years.

On September 5, 1986, the Tri-County Metropolitan Transportation District of Oregon (TriMet) opened its first light rail line. Now part of the MAX (Metropolitan Area eXpress) system, the Blue Line operates on an essentially east–west route from Gresham to Hillsboro. That portion of the line serving Northeast Portland, known as Eastside MAX, was part of the Banfield Light Rail Project funded with money originally intended for freeway expansion. At 33 miles, this is TriMet's longest line, and it includes portions of historic streetcar rights-of-way as it crosses the Steel Bridge and travels along East Burnside Street.

Over the years, MAX has operated more than 150 LRVs (light rail vehicles) in six variations. The Type 1 cars manufactured by Bombardier are now being phased out. LRV types 2-6 are all manufactured by Siemens.

The Portland Streetcar System started on July 20, 2001. It was the first new streetcar system using modern cars to open in the United States since World War II. Unlike the heavier-duty MAX Light Rail network, Portland Streetcar represents a return to more traditional smaller trolleys that share the street with automobile and truck traffic. Portland Streetcars are operated and maintained by TriMet but owned by the City of Portland and managed by a non-profit corporation. They share a goal with their historic streetcar predecessors in that lines are built with commercial development in mind.

Portland Streetcar operates two lines, the 4-mile NS (North South) Line links Northwest Portland neighborhoods to Portland State University and the South Waterfront. The now-6-mile Loop Line opened in September 2012 as a 4.5-mile route named the CL (Central Loop) Line, which used 3.3 miles of new route across the Broadway Bridge and through the Central Eastside Industrial District to OMSI and used existing tracks of the NS Line in Downtown. It was extended in September 2015 back across the river via the then-new Tilikum Crossing, which it shares with MAX trains.

As of mid-2024, Portland Streetcar has twenty-three cars, including three new cars not yet in service. Although similar in appearance, they were built by four different manufacturers. All are modern, low floor, articulated cars and all but the three newest were designed in the Czech Republic.

Seven of the Portland Streetcars were built in the Portland area by United Streetcar under license from Skoda. Unfortunately, United Streetcar proved unable to compete with foreign manufacturers and ceased production in 2014. United Streetcar was the only U.S. company building modern streetcars until 2013, when the torch passed to Brookville Equipment Corporation in Pennsylvania, who built the latest Portland Streetcars in 2022–2023.

On November 29, 1991, the non-profit Portland Vintage Trolley began a heritage streetcar service using four replica streetcars built in Iowa by the Gomaco Trolley Company. Their design is based on classic 1904 Brills used on Portland's iconic Council Crest Line.

The Vintage Trolley idea was promoted by businessman Bill Naito, who was instrumental in forming a local improvement district to lure shoppers back to the central city. His dream was supported by the Portland Landmarks Commission who sought to reduce the clash of modern LRVs running through historic Old Town.

VT operated over MAX tracks between the Lloyd District and downtown until 2009, when the route shifted to the Downtown Transit Mall. On July 6, 2014, VT succumbed to financial pressure and routing challenges and ceased operation. Two of its streetcars now operate on the Loop Trolley in St. Louis. The other two went to the Oregon Electric Railway Historical Society's Willamette Shore Trolley in Lake Oswego, where one has been converted to battery operation.

Eastside MAX & Streetcar Routes

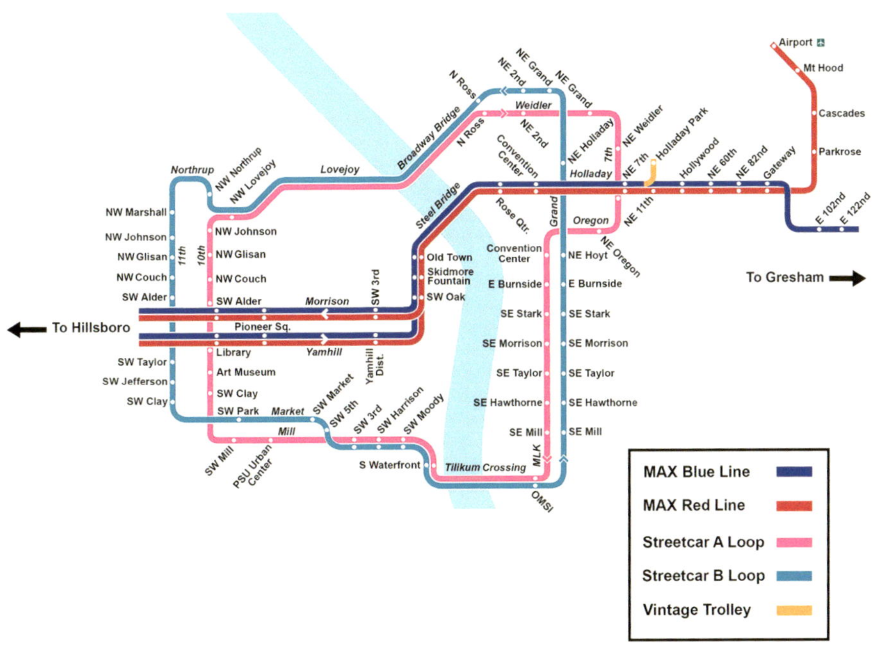

Above left: On Saturday, September 6, 1986, the second day of MAX service, one of two cars decorated with a "V" of flowers for the opening ceremonies pulls into Lloyd Center station. Throngs of eager riders fill the station platform, and people attempting to board are having trouble finding any space on board cars 101 and 109. (*Photograph by Steve Morgan*)

Above right: Just one station to the west, on the same day as the previous picture, the NE 7th Avenue station was looking comparatively quiet, probably because this area was occupied mostly by office buildings at that time. A train of Bombardier light rail vehicles led by No. 112 is westbound on NE Holladay Street between 9th and 7th Avenues. What was then the Red Lion Inn is in the background. (*Photograph by Steve Morgan*)

Much of the first MAX line ran in a relatively "un-streetcar-like" setting along the Banfield Freeway. In this photo taken on the MAX system's opening day a Gresham-bound train is seen from the 28th Avenue overpass. The former Doernbecher Manufacturing Company building at left, promoted as "the biggest furniture factory in the world," were once served by a streetcar stub line. (*Photograph by Steve Morgan*)

With the opening of the Oregon Convention Center on September 21, 1990, a new MAX station on Holladay Street was built. On the center's grand opening weekend, an inbound MAX train led by No. 104 pulls into the new station on September 23, 1990. Compare this scene with the photograph on page 128 taken at almost the same location thirty-four years later. (*Photograph by Steve Morgan*)

The Vintage Trolley service that began operation in 1991 used MAX tracks for all except its eastern terminal on NE 11th Avenue. On the first day of service, November 29, 1991, car 514 turns onto the VT-only single-track spur from Holladay Street. Its distinctive current collector was designed to be compatible with the modern MAX system's overhead wires but to have an older look. (*Photograph by Steve Morgan*)

Vintage Trolley 512 is seen in the VT Barn on May 2, 1992, in front of a barely visible Unimog road-rail vehicle. Ther Vintage Trolley carbarn was located beneath the I-5 freeway on NE Holladay Street and 1st Avenue. After the demise of the heritage streetcar operation tracks to this carbarn were removed and it was converted to a TriMet maintenance facility. (*Photograph by the author*)

Vintage Trolley 511 is eastbound turning from NE Holladay Street onto the spur track on 11th Avenue in 1992. The Red Lion Hotel in the background is now a DoubleTree. Each of the four Vintage Trolleys had a sponsor name painted on the side of the car. They were 511 U.S. Bank, 512 Portland General Electric, 513 Lloyd Center, and 514 Zell Brothers. (*Photograph by the author*)

Cars 249 and 220 are at the Airport terminal of the MAX Red Line on opening day, September 10, 2001. The following day, the terrorist attacks in New York closed all U.S. airports for three days and the big opening celebration for the new line was canceled, but the Red Line eventually became busy, with single cars replaced by two-car trains on heavy travel dates. (*Photograph by Steve Morgan*)

In order to reduce construction costs, two sections of the Red Line included bi-directional single track (an operations inconvenience that TriMet had eliminated on its Gresham line in 1996). Car 242, one of fifty-two Siemens SD660 low-floor LRVs acquired in 1996–2000, is approaching the airport along Airport Way on July 29, 2002. Most Red Line service used single cars until 2005. (*Photograph by Steve Morgan*)

Just east of the airport, the Red Line passed through an undeveloped area that would eventually be developed as the Cascade Station shopping mall. Meanwhile, until 2006, this section offered an unobstructed view of Mount Hood, Oregon's tallest peak. LRV 212 is airport-bound on July 20, 2003. Note the airplane pictogram on the car's rollsign. (*Photograph by Steve Morgan*)

TriMet Type 2 LRV 246, a 1998 Siemens SD660, pulls away from Parkrose/Sumner station in the median of I-205 in September 2002. New rollsigns purchased for the Red Line's opening have now replaced "Portland" with "City Center," although Portland's city center is invariably called "downtown" by the area's residents. (*Photograph by Steve Morgan*)

Above left: Traditional streetcars returned to Northeast Portland in 2012, with the Portland Streetcar's east-side line. Car 010, built in 2007 by Inekon Trams, is making the very first test trip over the new line (note "Testing" on its sign), on February 21, 2012. It is passing two traditional early twentieth-century houses on NE Weidler. (*Photograph by Steve Morgan*)

Above right: This second photo of No. 010 during the first test trip illustrates how the two colors worn by each streetcar are positioned differently on opposite sides of the car. No. 010 was westbound on Broadway at NE 2nd Avenue, passing Broadway Furniture. The furniture store moved to suburban Tigard in 2014, but its building on Broadway still stands today. (*Photograph by Steve Morgan*)

The east side line, initially known as the Central Loop or "CL Line," opened on September 22, 2012. Car 005, a 2001 Skoda/Inekon 10T, is southbound on 7th Avenue at Hassalo Street on the fifth day of service. Its LCD destination sign reads "OMSI via Lloyd [District]." This picture was taken on September 26 as the trees were starting to change color. (*Photograph by Steve Morgan*)

Streetcar 015 is westbound on Oregon Street on October 6, 2012, with the spires of the Oregon Convention Center towering in the background. The 2009-built prototype for streetcars built in the Portland area by United Streetcar carried "Made In USA" lettering on its sides. It was fitted with an experimental propulsion system, which proved unreliable, and the car was put up for sale in 2024. (*Photograph by Steve Morgan*)

Car 004 (a 2001-built Skoda) is southbound on NE 7th Avenue at Hassalo Street on September 23, 2012, the second day of service on the CL Line. It is passing the Temple Baptist Church. The original Scandinavian congregation dropped the word "Swedish" from their name in 1926. Although the neighborhood dates to the 1880s, PRL&P never had tracks here. (*Photograph by Steve Morgan*)

Northbound streetcar 022 is on Grand Avenue crossing the MAX tracks on Holladay Street during a February 8, 2014, snowstorm. No. 022 was one of six production-series streetcars built in the Clackamas area by United Streetcar in 2012–2014 following 2009 prototype 015. Unfortunately, financial troubles and a lack of orders led the small company to cease operating in 2015. (*Photograph by Steve Morgan*)

A westbound MAX Red Line train consisting of Siemens SD660 Type 2 and Type 3 cars 220 and 314 is pulling into the NE 7th Avenue station on June 20, 2015. By 2015, the construction of new high-rise apartment buildings had greatly altered the appearance of the NE 7th Avenue station from how the same location looked in the 1986 photo on page 116. (*Photograph by Steve Morgan*)

Part of the Red Line operates in the middle of the Interstate 205 freeway, as can be seen in this view looking south from Prescott Street on June 20, 2015. A train made of up low-floor LRV 237 and high-floor car 125 is southbound. The latter is wearing the new paint scheme TriMet adopted in 2002, which is also when the agency's name was altered slightly from Tri-Met to TriMet. (*Photograph by Steve Morgan*)

The MAX Red Line moves from the median of Interstate 205 to the freeway's east side via a tunnel that was built during the freeway's construction in the early 1980s. The tunnel was built for a proposed future "transitway," which at the time was expected to be a busway but proved perfect for use by MAX. A train of Type 4 (Siemens S70) LRVs is southbound in 2015. (*Photograph by Steve Morgan*)

Streetcar 003, built by Skoda/Inekon in 2001, travels north on Grand Avenue at Holladay Street on the B Loop, a 2015 renaming of the counterclockwise version of what had been the CL Line. The tower of the former Sears store in the background is now the headquarters of the Portland area's regional government, Metro. (*Photograph by Steve Morgan*)

By 2015, MAX's Banfield Freeway section was being used by three light rail lines designated Blue, Green, and Red. In this photograph looking east from 60th Avenue in July 2017, the Union Pacific railroad track is at left and Rocky Butte in the background. Freeway congestion would undoubtedly be much heavier nowadays if not for the three MAX lines. (*Photograph by Steve Morgan*)

On September 6, 2015, car 246 is leading a two-car train of Siemens SD660 LRVs (one Type 2 and one Type 3) away from the airport, in two-way single track. The airport's control tower is visible in the distance. LED destination signs replaced rollsigns in all of the Type 1-3 LRVs in 2014–2016. (*Photograph by Steve Morgan*)

United Streetcar model 100 car 021 was decorated in late 2022 with a Holiday-Season-themed "wrap" celebrating the tradition of mailing of gifts and greeting cards and featuring Portland's famous White Stag Sign (an official Portland Historic Landmark). It was photographed turning onto Martin Luther King Jr. Blvd. from Oregon Street, on the "A Loop" line on December 18, 2022. (*Photograph by Steve Morgan*)